Studies and documents on cultural policies

Recent titles in this series:

For a complete list of titles see page 87

# Cultural policy in
# Czechoslovakia

**Milan Šimek and
Jaroslav Dewetter**

**Unesco**

First published in 1970 by the United Nations Educational,
Scientific and Cultural Organization,
7 Place de Fontenoy, 75700 Paris
Printed by Imprimerie des Presses Universitaires de France,
Vendôme

Second edition 1986

ISBN 92-3-102360-8

# Preface

The purpose of this series is to show how cultural policies are planned and implemented in various Member States.

As cultures differ, so does the approach to them; it is for each Member State to determine its cultural policy and methods according to its own conception of culture, its socio-economic system, political ideology and technical development. However, the methods of cultural policy (like those of general development policy) have certain common problems; these are largely institutional, administrative and financial in nature, and the need has increasingly been stressed for exchanging experiences and information about them. This series, each issue of which follows as far as possible a similar pattern so as to make comparison easier, is mainly concerned with these technical aspects of cultural policy.

In general, the studies deal with the principles and methods of cultural policy, the evaluation of cultural needs, administrative structures and management, planning and financing, the organization of resources, legislation, budgeting, public and private institutions, cultural content in education, cultural autonomy and decentralization, the training of personnel, institutional infrastructures for meeting specific cultural needs, the safeguarding of the cultural heritage, institutions for the dissemination of the arts, international cultural co-operation and other related subjects.

The studies, which cover countries belonging to differing social and economic systems, geographical areas and levels of development, present therefore a wide variety of approaches and methods in cultural policy. Taken as a whole, they can provide guidelines to countries which have yet to establish cultural policies, while all countries, especially those seeking new formulations of such policies, can profit by the experience already gained.

This study was prepared for Unesco by Milan Šimek and Jaroslav Dewetter of the Institute for the Research of Culture, Prague. It was commissioned by Unesco to bring up to date an earlier publication of the same title, which was issued in 1970.

The authors are responsible for the choice and the presentation of the facts contained in this book and for the opinions expressed therein, which are not necessarily those of Unesco and do not commit the Organization.

# Contents

## Introductory note

The Czechoslovak Socialist Republic is a federative state consisting of the Czech Socialist Republic and the Slovak Socialist Republic.

In 1984, Czechoslovakia had a total population of 15,437,038, with 10,328,221 living in the Czech Socialist Republic and 5,108,817 in the Slovak Socialist Republic.

Out of the total population, 9,805,000 were Czechs and 4,769,000 Slovaks. The national minorities consisted of 585,000 Hungarians, 70,000 Poles, 60,000 Germans and 47,000 Ukrainians.

Both Republics are subdivided into regions and districts. The Czech Socialist Republic has an area of 78,864 km² and the Slovak Socialist Republic of 49,035 km².

# Culture in the history
# of the nations of Czechoslovakia
# from ancient times

The first historical accounts of the territory on which the Czechoslovak Socialist Republic is situated today are contained in Roman records. After the victorious war of the Emperor Trajan against the Dacian king Decebalus, the frontiers of the Roman Empire were extended during the first and second centuries A.D. as far as the north bank of the Danube, so that even today there still exist in southern Slovakia and southern Moravia a number of monuments bearing witness to the presence of Roman legions. The capital of the Slovak Socialist Republic, Bratislava, was at that time in a key position for the Romans.

The Latin name 'Bohemia' is derived from the name of one of the Celtic tribes that settled during the fourth and third centuries B.C. in these regions (The Boii—Boichemum—Bohemia). At the time of the disintegration of the Roman Empire and during the migration of the peoples, German tribes (the Marcomanni, the Goths and the Quadi) settled in turn on the territory of Bohemia, Moravia and Slovakia; and after the relatively brief episode of the Hun incursion on the territory of today's Slovakia, Slav tribes settled there between the fifth and the tenth centuries A.D. The Slavs did not encounter the Romans, for the Roman frontier already belonged to the distant past, nor did they suffer greatly from contact with the German Visigoths, Ostrogoths and Longobards, but for a short time they came under the rule of the Avars, a people of Tartar origin, from whose bondage they extricated themselves under the leadership of the Frankish merchant Samo. He established the first supra-tribal formation in this area, an alliance of tribes known as the Samo Empire. The centre of this empire was Wogatisburg, but historians have never succeeded in locating it. According to varying sources, it could have been in Bohemia or Moravia, or even to the west of the Bohemian Forest, because the Slav settlement at one time reached as far as the Saale River. After Samo's death, his empire disintegrated. It had existed from 623 to 659 A.D.

## The first script, the first university

In spite of its relatively short duration, the most important period of the Slav settlement of this part of Europe was the Great Moravian Empire (830–907). This first state came into existence in a complicated political situation where the interests of the east Frankish Empire, the process of Christianization, the interests of the Pope and those of the Byzantine Emperor in Constantinople were in conflict. Since Bohemia belonged to the Ratisbon bishopric, and Moravia and Slovakia to the Passau bishopric, the adoption of Christianity was necessarily connected with the consolidation of German influence; thus a hard struggle by Great Moravia began for the establishment and recognition of an independent ecclesiastical administration, and of a separate diocese, independent of the Bavarian episcopate. The Great Moravian Prince, Ratislav, made this request to Pope Nicolas I, who refused to grant it because of Louis the Frank, and also because he had at that time in Rome neither a Slav bishop nor Slav priests. Ratislav then sent a delegation with a similar demand to the Byzantine Emperor, Michael III, in 862. As a result, a mission came to Moravia which had a deep impact on the life of the Slav nations. It was headed by two brothers from Thessalonika, from a Slav family, who were among the most capable men available to the Emperor. They were Cyril (his proper name being Constantine) who had worked until then as a missionary, first with the Khazars in the area of the Caspian Sea, and later with his brother Methodius with the Bulgarians, where he compiled the first Slavonic script—the Glagolitic. In Moravia, the brothers, together with their pupils, continued to translate biblical texts and at the same time worked as teachers and lawyers. They became thus not only the founders of Slavonic literature and the creators of the literary Slavonic language, but also of the Slavonic educational system and law (code for the lay people). Thanks to them, the Slavs were the first people in medieval Europe to have their own literary language (after Hebrew, Greek and Latin), the first literature and the first code being written in the Slavonic language. They also introduced the Slavonic language into the liturgy, established an independent ecclesiastical organization and finally achieved its approval by Pope Hadrian II. Methodius became the first bishop of the Pannonian–Moravian diocese (his brother having died in the meantime). Archaeological discoveries at Staré Město, Nitra, Mikulčice and other localities have revealed the economic and cultural maturity of this state.

The power of the Great Moravian Empire came to an end under Prince Svatopluk. After his death, the empire disintegrated in heavy fighting and its eastern part, including Slovakia, became a part of Hungary. For a millennium Slovakia was ethnically, linguistically and culturally connected with Bohemia and Moravia, but politically subordinate to Hungary. This situation continued until the creation of an independent Czechoslovak state in 1918.

In Bohemia, it was the Přemyslid dynasty that assumed power and constituted the Czech state. Under their reign, the political and cultural importance of the Czech state gradually increased. The Prague bishopric was established in 943, and in 1212 the King's title and the right to elect the Holy Roman Emperor were granted hereditarily to the Czech monarch through the Sicilian Golden Bull. The western territories of the Great Moravian Empire were annexed to the kingdom of Bohemia as the margravate of Moravia. After five centuries of rule by the Přemyslid dynasty, in the fourteenth century under the reign of the Luxemburgian Charles IV a flowering of art and science took place and Prague, capital of the Holy Roman Empire, became also one of the most outstanding European cultural centres. Among the many acts of historical significance by this ruler was the foundation of the University in 1348, one of the first institutes of higher learning north of the Alps.

On the territory which is now Czechoslovakia, many styles of art, beginning with the Romanesque, gradually developed. Typical of the Romanesque period on Czech as well as Slovak territory, are buildings of the basilica and particularly the rotunda type, and richly illuminated manuscripts. A unique example of the architecture of the period is Spiš Castle in Slovakia.

From the thirteenth until the middle of the sixteenth century, Czech and Slovak art witnessed the flowering of the Gothic style. It had contact alternately with French, Italian and (in the course of the fifteenth century) Dutch art. Czech Gothic art, linked through medieval universalism with the whole world of that time, found through its most important works its own means of expression. In the early Gothic period, the most famous works are the desk paintings by the Master of the Vyšší Brod cycle and the wooden ornamental sculptures of South Bohemian madonnas. Gothic art developed intensively under the Luxemburgians in the second half of the fourteenth century when it attained world renown, came into contact with humanistic trends (Petrarch) and, in the sphere of visual art, reached its culmination. In the reign of Charles IV and Wenceslas IV, there were in Bohemia some of the greatest figures in European art, for example, Matthias of Arras, Petr Parléř and his workshop, and Master Theodoricus, who created the Krumlov Madonna. The greatest figure of Gothic art in Slovakia is Master Pavol z Levoče. Czech visual art participated in the solution of problems in iconography, monumental ornamental sculptures, portrait-painting, landscape-painting and painting technique. All these efforts led to the so-called 'beautiful style' which is the specific expression of the Czech conception of the visual arts at that time. Arts and crafts also achieved a high level during that period.

The culminating Gothic style is also to be found in architecture, although not many original buildings have been preserved. The best known are castles such as Zvíkov, Karlštejn, Pernštejn, middle-class houses at Kremnica in Slovakia, a number of churches, among them the unique St Vitus'

Cathedral within the precincts of the Late Gothic St Martin's Cathedral in
Bratislava; the Prague Charles Bridge, and the unique urban plan of
Prague New Town that has remained until now, in its original form,
the centre of Prague.

There was a Czech literary language and sacerdotal literature (liturgical)
as early as the eleventh century. From the thirteenth century Czech was
also used in secular works, where it gradually replaced Latin. The richly
illuminated manuscripts are another example of a high level of visual art.
Music had been developing since the ninth century, first for ecclesiastical
use, with secular music developing only in the thirteenth century.

Among the most important figures of the period was Jan (John) Hus,
rector of Prague University, a religious thinker and reformer whose ideas
became the basis of the Hussite revolution. His predecessors in the religious
reform movement in Bohemia were first aroused in the reign of Charles IV
by Jan Milíč z Kroměříže. They were connected with the ecclesiastical
movement, Devotio Moderna, and with the gradual decay of medieval
society reflected in philosophy, in the disintegration of ecclesiastical
organization, and in the discrepancies between the Church and secular
power, between the nobility and the ruler, and the nobility and the middle
classes, between town and country, and also, within the Church, between
the poor and the rich clergy. The contradictory ideological currents crossed
one another at Prague University, particularly in the controversy over
Viklef's ideas. The condemnation in 1415 of Jan Hus by the Council,
and his death at the stake because he refused to accept the authority of
the Church and to abjure his convictions, were considered in Bohemia an
outrage upon the nation, and the majority of the people were united in
opposing the Roman Curia as well as the ruler. The idea of replacing
the Church by God's people had already been preached in Bohemia by
Milíč and spread far beyond the pulpits, turning into an impressive people's
revolutionary and social movement which did not hesitate to take up
arms to defend its truth. Under the leadership of Jan Žižka z Trocnova and
of his successor, the priest Prokop Holý, Hussite armies repeatedly defeated
for twelve years the armies of crusaders who tried with their formidable
and superior forces to subjugate the 'heretical' nation. This movement in the
national history became a mighty ideological force, a heritage which
strengthened the nation for centuries in its struggle for existence and social
justice. The Reformation had, as its predecessor, the Hussite revolution.

In Bohemia and Moravia, at the time of the Reformation, there emerged
some quite exceptional cultural figures—Petr Chelčický, a religious
thinker and social Utopian, Jan Amos Komenský (Comenius), a pedagogical
reformer of world renown, the engraver Václav Hollar, the lawyer and
politician Pavel Stránský, author of works on the Czech state, and many
others.

King Jiří z Poděbrad (George of Poděbrady) was clearly ahead of
his time, with a broad outlook which extended beyond his own region.

In 1464, he sent a delegation to the King of France with a proposal for a peace conference of European countries. His aims live still in the idea of European security and of the peaceful solution of the problems of international politics. Because of the influence of the Czech state, Czech became for a certain time the diplomatic language, even in Hungary and Poland.

At this time, humanist literature also developed and the unique Kralice Bible was produced which preserved the high level of the Czech language until the national revival at the beginning of the nineteenth century.

The Reformation and the humanistic trends influenced the growth of general education, which was a remarkable achievement at that time. In the fifteenth and sixteenth centuries, at least half the population of Bohemia and Moravia were literate, which was unique for the period. Ernest Denis, Professor at the Sorbonne and a great expert in Czech history, mentions in this connection the extraordinarily rapid development of printing in Bohemia and Moravia. Czech printed books were among the first in Europe; the demand for them was so great that the output of local printers was insufficient, and Czech books had to be printed in Germany and Italy as well. 'At that time, perhaps no other nation in Europe was taken up with such a desire to read and to know; nowhere is the mental and moral life so strong, schools so numerous and so well administered', writes Ernest Denis.

## The Counter-Reformation

With the Defenestration of Prague in 1618 began the Thirty Years War, and in the Battle of the White Mountain in 1620 the Czechs were defeated and the regions under the Czech crown lost their independence. The Catholic religion was reimposed and there was also a policy of Germanization, the Czech language being excluded from public life. However, military and political defeat and the oppression ensuing from it did not prevent cultural development. The national struggle was, on the contrary, transferred to the cultural sphere. After a relatively short period of Renaissance art (exemplified by palaces in Bohemia and bourgeois houses in Slovakia) came the Czech Baroque, which expressed through architecture, sculpture, painting, music and poetry, as well as folk art, unique interpretation of Baroque art.

It was natural that this unprecedented unity should be found in Prague, a city where different cultural, artistic and ideological currents met. The work of architects such as Christopher and Kilian Ignatius Dienzenhofer, Giovanni Santini, Francesco Caratti and František Maxmilián Kaňka, of sculptors such as Matthias Bernard Braun and Ferdinand Maxmilián Brokov, and of painters such as Petr Jan Brandl and Karel Škréta, were inspired by the skill of many ordinary folk artists, unknown today, whose anonymous works, typical of the heritage of our country, can be seen in our churches and castles.

## The national revival

It was only at the end of the eighteenth and the beginning of the nineteenth century that conditions were ripe for the revival of national feeling. The population flow from the country to the towns intensified this emotion amongst intellectuals too, and encouraged them to join the struggle for the revival of the nation. This was period of enlightenment and of the French Revolution, which encouraged the democratic character of the revival and led, in the memorable year of 1848, to a revolutionary uprising, which was suppressed by military force.

This revival started at the time of the attempt of Joseph II to denationalize public life in Bohemia, Moravia and Slovakia, an attempt which inspired progressive teachers and priests to strive for the preservation of the national identity. Thus, at first, the revival was concerned with culture and language. In the countryside, amateur theatricals came into existence; in Prague, the first Czech newspaper started to appear regularly, with the aim of propagating among the people the educational and scientific discoveries of that time (in fact the very first periodical was in Czech and had been published for several years from as early as 1597) ; and at Charles University the study of the Czech language recommenced in 1792. In 1818, the first people's library came into existence in Bohemia. In the same year, the Museum of the Kingdom of Bohemia was founded and its scientific journal, which began publication in 1827, still exists. The development of the modern literary language in Bohemia and Moravia owes much to J. Dobrovský and J. Jungmann; in Slovakia, to A. Bernolák and especially to L. Štúr, whose endeavours culminated in 1843 in the codification of the Slovak literary language. Two Slovak scientists and poets, Jan Kollár and Pavel Jozef Šafařik, were of great importance in arousing the national consciousness in the broader context of the Slav nations. In the following period, the cultural movement spread to many corporations and special-interest associations, for already, more than a hundred years ago, an important role was played by the workers' educational and readers' associations. It should be emphasized that the national revival had a purely democratic character and its representatives, many of whom attained an important position in scientific and artistic milieux, all came from humble backgrounds. This influenced the further development of Czech and Slovak culture and was strikingly expressed in revolutionary, social and national struggles in the nineteenth century.

Towards the end of the First World War, the Austro-Hungarian Empire disintegrated. From its ashes, several independent states emerged, among them Czechoslovakia. The new state consisted of Bohemia, Moravia, part of Silesia and Slovakia. In spite of the affinities of language and culture, it was necessary to solve the problems arising from different socio-historical and socio-economic conditions. Further progress put Czechoslovakia among the most highly developed European countries, culturally and economically. The period between the two world wars was, at the same time, marked by the struggle for the character of the state. An important role in the political and cultural life of the country was played by the Communist Party, founded in 1921, whose ideological authority attracted prominent artists and cultural workers to socialism. The decisive influence in cultural life at that time was that of the groups of progressive artists, such as Devětsil, DAV and the Left Front. In the critical years of the emergence of Fascism, Czech and Slovak cultural workers united in taking up the cause of progress and many of them (for example, V. Vančura, J. Fučik and B. Václavek) sacrificed their lives in the struggle.

### Socialist culture

The Second World War and the occupation were a test of the inner strength of Czech and Slovak culture. In prose, poetry and drama, progressive artists aroused the spirit of the nation. Some of their works appeared in the illegal press. When the famous Slovak National Uprising against the occupying forces began, words by prominent Slovak literary, musical and dramatic artists as well as satirical programmes resounded from the radio transmitter at Banská Bystrica. On liberated territory, Soviet films were projected and the Front Theatre performed, headed by the national artist A. Bagar.

The revolt and partisan movement which developed on Czech territories, culminated in the uprising of the Czech people in May 1945. After the liberation of Czechoslovakia by the Soviet Army in 1945, and the restoration of the state as a union of two nations with equal rights—the Czechs and the Slovaks—attention was focused on the most important aspects of building socialist culture. This trend was confirmed, after the successful socialist revolution in February 1948, by the representative Congress of National Culture. Its meaning and its programme were depicted explicitly and truthfully by the then President of the Republic, Klement Gottwald, in his speech:

We start today a great planned drive not only for the economic but also the cultural renewal of the people. In order to renew man spiritually and morally, we wish to make all the great cultural treasures of the past accessible to him and to throw wide open for him the door to knowledge and beauty. It is not only a matter of making existing culture accessible, our people also need a new culture of today, living today and contributing to today.

The programme emphasized the necessity of making the entire heritage of national as well as world culture accessible to an ever-increasing extent, also the importance of cultural orientation in the building of a socialist society.

Transformations in the whole structure of society and in the cultural life of the people took place. Among the greatest successes in the sphere of culture have been the completion of the system of uniform public education, of the network of state theatres, cinemas and libraries, of the organization of press, radio and television, of museums and galleries, and of the film and record industry. New organizations and institutions, important in the sphere of science and art, came into being, the first being the Czech Academy of Sciences and the Slovak Academy of Sciences.

One of the most important and topical tasks of socialist cultural policy was the abolition of differences between the cultural level and possibilities for cultural life of the population in the Czech region and the Slovak region. These were due to the consequences of history, Slovakia having been mostly an agrarian territory, whilst in Bohemia and Moravia industry had been effectively developing since the beginning of the nineteenth century. This imbalance has been successfully corrected, thanks to a purposeful and highly principled national policy. During the short period of existence of socialist Czechoslovakia, differences in cultural level have disappeared. Today, Slovakia has the same rich culture: its public education system and its artistic production are of a high level, the Slovak Philharmonic Orchestra and National Gallery have come into existence, as well as a dense network of cultural facilities and scientific institutions.

The development of socialism in Czechoslovakia gradually brought new tasks and problems. In their solution, demands on the cultural and political as well as the cultural and educational function of the state also increased. More and more importance is attached to culture, which plays a growing role in the overall social and economic development of the country, and in the present policy for both art and education, creative activity, the culture of the working and human environment, and the whole socialist life-style. The cultural policy permeates the activity of practically all cultural branches, and thus contributes significantly to the shaping of the socialistically conscious, politically minded, all-round personality of the citizens and to the cultivation and development of their creative forces, capacities and skills. It helps to form their practical opinions, attitudes and value orientations. Through its long-term and purposeful orientation it permits the maximum exploitation of all the available values of national and world culture, and, at the same time, it stimulates and directs the process of creation of new values which enrich the national culture as well as the life of Czechoslovak citizens. Citizens of the Czechoslovak Socialist Republic are no longer mere recipients of culture and education, they are becoming to an increasing extent active participants and creators of cultural values.

# Czechoslovak art

The Czech and Slovak cultures have played an extraordinary role in the history of both nations. After the loss of independence they were the guardians of the national conscience, and when the country was reborn they helped in a decisive way to revive the national sense of identity.

The tradition of portraying socially important ideas, progress and freedom, not only for our own nation but also for all mankind, has been maintained by Czech and Slovak art up to the present day. It has never experienced narrow nationalism but has always been open to the whole world. This tradition, accompanied by profound democratic feeling, continues to be a source of permanent inspiration for all developments in Czechoslovak art and links it with the art of the whole world.

## Literature

The country's most ancient existing manuscripts are written in Old Slavonic, and from the eleventh century onwards in Latin. Also in the eleventh century, Czech was used for the first time in literature. In the following centuries, lyric and epic poetry, legends, tales of chivalry and satire developed.

The philosophical and religious works of the predecessors of Jan Hus, and his own writings as well, mark an important stage in the development of Czech literature. The flowering of individual genres took place in the sixteenth century, when the translation of the Scriptures (the so-called Kralice Bible) considerably influenced the development of the literary language.

During the Counter-Reformation, there was a considerable decline in the quality of writing. New developments began only at the turn of the eighteenth and nineteenth centuries when the specific literatures of the Czech and Slovak nations began to emerge, at first inspired by other European

17

literary sources and by memories of national songs (V. Thám, A. J. Puch-majer, the prominent linguist J. Jungmann, J. Kollár, P. J. Šafárik, F. L. Čelakovský, etc.). Later, work of greater maturity came from the pen of K. H. Mácha, who anticipated a new era in Czech literature and who had a great influence on the further development of *belles-lettres* for several generations. Czech and Slovak literature either dealt with the glorious past of both nations, Panslavism, etc., or with the folklore tradition. The works of B. Němcová, J. Neruda, A. Jirásek, J. Botto, S. Chalupka, etc., continue to enjoy great success and, for example, *The Grandmother* by B. Němcová has been translated into twenty-nine languages.

The literature of small nations is closely linked with the literary activity of other countries, and for this reason the Czechs and the Slovaks have been seeking a way of incorporating the values of world literature into local literary life. Translations have thus not only had an informative role, but have always been considered as literature which enriches intellectually and inspires the national literary production. Shakespeare was performed on the Czech stage for the first time in 1786, and by the middle of the nineteenth century all his works were available in Czech. Translation was undertaken at that time by the most prominent writers, such as J. Jungmann, F. L. Čelakovský, J. V. Sládek and J. Vrchlický who considered it an important artistic activity. In the twentieth century prominent poets and writers, such as K. Čapek, J. Hora, S. K. Neumann, V. Nezval, J. Seifert, J. Jesenský and P. Jilemnický, have devoted themselves to translation; specialized translators, such as E. A. Saudek, O. Fisher and B. Mathesius, try not only to translate but, by means of poetic language and all its possibilities of expression, to create a work faithful to the author and at the same time meaningful for our time.

Many Czech and Slovak writers have also worked as journalists, and through the press they have directly influenced public opinion. They have not only raised Czech and Slovak journalism to a high literary level, but also enriched the literary language with new means of expression. K. Havlíček Borovský, J. Neruda, K. Čapek, F. Langer, M. Majerová, I. Olbracht, E. Bass, K. Poláček, V. Vančura and J. Fučík played a direct part in the struggle for national and social progress.

At the turn of the nineteenth and twentieth centuries Czech and Slovak literature was of such a high quality that works by some writers penetrated the European consciousness. Among these writers were O. Březina, a symbolist poet with the concentration and pathos of a great thinker, and P. Bezruč, the bard of rebellion against social and national oppression. K. Čapek became, between the two world wars, an author of world reputation, particularly for his deeply humanist philosophy, consistent anti-Fascism and his anticipation of the serious problems resulting from the technical civilization. Poetry between the wars reached a high level with the works of S. K. Neumann, J. Wolker, V. Nezval, Nobel Prize Laureate J. Seifert, J. Hora, F. Halas and other authors. However, their work has penetrated only slowly and uneasily into the consciousness of other nations, because it contains values that can be translated only with difficulty into another language. The world-famous work by the Czech author, J. Hašek, *The Good Soldier Schweik*, was translated in the 1920s into German and French, and at the same time was dramatized and staged in Berlin by E. Piscator. After the Second World War, in new historical contexts, it experienced great popularity, and today has been translated into more than thirty languages.

Modern Slovak literature, since the turn of the century, has absorbed the progressive aspects of European literature and shaped them into a specific national form. Mention should be made of I. Krasko, J. Smrek, F. Král, L. Novomeský and M. Figuli. The realistic current was to be seen in the socialist realism of F. Král and P. Jilemnický.

Post-war Czech and Slovak writers became known for their poetry, which after the hard years of the occupation praised the new peaceful life and gave thanks to the liberators, while at the same time warning of the dangers of atomic war. The main poets were V. Holan, F. Hrubín, V. Nezval, J. Seifert, V. Závada, L. Novomeský, Š. Žáry and J. Smrek. Czech and Slovak prose treated such subjects as individual and collective heroism and post-war reconstruction. Among the famous authors were J. Drda, V. Řezáč, M. Pujmanová, N. Frýd, R. Jašík and V. Mináč.

Since then, poetry and prose have treated an increasing range of topics. Intimate personal relationships, domestic problems, the struggle for peace and other important social problems, are the main subjects of Czech and Slovak poetry represented by authors such as J. Kainar, I. Skála, M. Florian, M. Válek, M. Lajčiak and V. Mihálik.

Prose works with a topical socio-political content, and psychological studies of the human psyche have been published (J. Otčenášek, Z. Pluhař, P. Jaroš, L. Ballek), also historical works (V. Neff, F. Kožík, M. V. Kratochvíl, J. Toman, A. Pludek), science fiction (J. Nesvadba, L. Smrek) and novels describing contemporary man and his creative attitude to life (J. Kozák, B. Říha, J. Fuchs, V. Páral, B. Hrabal, J. Marek, J. Kot, J. Jonáš, etc.).

At present there is a new generation of young poets and prose writers emerging in Czech and Slovak literature.

Translations from foreign languages constitute a quarter of the 7,000 book titles published every year. They are printed in a total number of almost 100 million copies (this is almost three-quarters of the total number of copies of books published in Czechoslovakia). During the last five years, almost 1,900 titles of foreign fiction have been published (360 titles from the Anglo-Saxon countries, 210 titles from French-speaking countries, 300 titles from German-speaking countries and 690 from the Russian). The print run of some books often greatly exceeds that in the author's own country. More than 70 per cent of households have a library of more than 100 books (this percentage is increasing), the network of scientific and public libraries, administered by the state, contains about 70 million books, and fourteen readers' clubs have about 1,351,000 members all of which demonstrates the important role played by literature in the life of the nations of Czechoslovakia.

The Artia Publishing House has contacts with prominent European and overseas publishing houses. Czechoslovak books for export cover the fields of literature on art (in first place), children's literature and educational literature. There is also a great interest in cartography, newspapers and periodicals (Artia exports about 600 titles yearly), in Czech and Slovak textbooks and in illustrated works on Czechoslovakia, its natural beauties, cultural and historical monuments. The high level of book production is demonstrated also by the quality of the illustrations by prominent Czechoslovak painters, graphic artists and photographers which are an integral part of the volumes. Among the most successful publishing projects of the Artia Publishing House are such series as 'World Art', 'Czech Art', 'World Drawing', 'Artist's Workshop', 'World Fairy-tales', 'String of Pearls' and 'From Fairy-tale to Fairy-tale', or books such as *Primeval Man* and *Primeval Nature* with masterly illustrations by Z. Burian, etc. Czechoslovak books have won numerous prizes at book fairs in Frankfurt-on-Main, Moscow, Nice, Leipzig and Poznan.

## Drama

Drama in the Czech and Slovak nations started to develop in Latin in the twelfth century and in Czech in the thirteenth when secular subjects began to replace liturgical themes. The Hussite movement rejected the theatre and it was revived only after a long interval in the sixteenth century. During the Counter-Reformation, Czech theatre existed only in the countryside, while in the towns mostly foreign theatrical companies performed mainly in German.

The professional Czech theatre came into existence only at the beginning of the national revival and, together with literature, it occupies the most important position in the national culture. Many itinerant dramatic societies travelled from village to village and from town to town spreading consciousness of the national identity and the culture of the literary language. A legendary figure of this period is J. K. Tyl, a many-sided talent—a writer, playwright, journalist, actor and producer. Some of his plays are still performed at the National Theatre in Prague which was built in the years 1868–83, the expenses being covered mostly from the people's donations. National and social themes formed the content of Slovak dramatic literature as well, J. G. Tajovský, for example.

For the development of Slovak dramatic art, the foundation of the Slovak National Theatre in Bratislava in 1919 was of great importance. It was followed by other professional theatres. Since the beginning of modern

TABLE 1.                    Theatre in Czechoslovakia, 1955–82

| Year | Number of theatres | Number of ensembles | Number of performances | Number of visitors (1,000s) | Number of visitors: index=100 |
|------|---------|---------|---------|---------|---------|
| 1955 | 70 | — | 26 230 | 12 749 | 100.00 |
| 1960 | 80 | 107 | 27 738 | 12 762 | 100.10 |
| 1965 | 84 | 103 | 24 258 | 10 418 | 81.72 |
| 1970 | 83 | 105 | 22 016 | 9 486 | 74.41 |
| 1975 | 85 | 105 | 22 094 | 9 566 | 75.03 |
| 1980 | 80 | 105 | 21 890 | 8 732 | 68.49 |
| 1981 | 82 | 103 | 21 925 | 8 704 | 68.27 |
| 1982 | 81 | 103 | 21 793 | 8 683 | 68.11 |
| 1983 | 83 | 103 | 21 709 | 8 627 | 67.66 |

theatre, part of the repertory has been devoted to a selection from world-famous classical and recent dramatic literature. Plays have been produced according to great directors' styles, combining Czech and Slovak stage art with current world developments, and reacting very sensitively to all their innovations. Thus, in the twentieth century, the drama far exceeds the former programme of national revival, and thanks to the creative work of personalities such as K. H. Hilar, J. Kvapil, J. Borodáč, J. Jamnický, J. Honzl, O. Stibor, J. Frejka and E. F. Burian, the stage has become the space where important artistic, philosophical and social problems are solved (see Table 1). Earlier dramatic productions focused on patriotic, historical themes, the life of the peasants or on more particular works of critical realism. This was in the period between the two world wars and the plays became known abroad. First, we should mention the work of Karel Čapek. From the 1920s, he wrote science fiction such as *R.U.R.*, dealing with robots (this word, which has become international, was coined by the author for this play). At the end of the 1930s he wrote the anti-war *Power and Glory* and, shortly afterwards, the story of *The Mother*, who reacts with a heroic gesture to the imminent menace to her country.

In the period between the two world wars, the formation of amateur stage groups began, some of which are developing into professional theatres. Even before the Second World War, quite a number of avant-garde theatres had come into existence, the most important being the Liberated Theatre, which developed from the constructivist experiments in staging the philosophical and political clowning of J. Voskovec and J. Werich in the form of a revue. There was a broad social response to this at the time that Fascism made its first appearance.

Anti-war plays were written after 1945. The best-known of these is Vítězslav Nezval's *Today the Sun Still Sets Above the Atlantida*, and also plays about post-war reconstruction, social conflicts and men at work (M. Stehlík, F. Hrubín). Further themes have been personal relationships,

21

relations between generations, subjects from history and contemporary life. Famous contemporary dramatists are O. Daněk, J. Šotola, J. Solovič, O. Zahradník and I. Bukovčan.

Apart from the main theatres such as the National and Tyl's theatres in Prague and the Slovak and Hviezdoslav's theatres in Bratislava, the significant theatrical work takes place in small theatres such as Nazábradlí (On the Railings) Theatre, Semafor (Semaphore) and others. There are about 150,000 inhabitants per professional theatre.

The healthy level of activity in Czechoslovak theatre can be gauged by the fact that in 1982, for example, theatre ensembles staged 568 premières, and 548 performances abroad.

The work of dramatic ensembles in co-operation with television, radio and the cinema has yielded results of international standard. For example, the Slovak National Theatre participated in 1982 in the festival of Schiller's works in Mannheim and the Prague J. Wolker Theatre took part in 1972 in the international festival of theatres for children and youth in Sofia. Some actors, directors and stage designers have achieved world recognition.

The professional theatre has to consider seriously the amateur movement whose main yearly display is the Jirásek Hronov. The ensembles which have attained a professional standard attract the attention of the public and professional critics through such displays, and later even sometimes reach the professional stage. These are mainly young groups for young audiences.

The Czech and Slovak opera is of a high level, as a result of its great composers and of singers such as E. and K. Burian, O. Mařák, A. Nordenová, E. Destinová, M. Veselá and many others who enjoyed great success at home and abroad. Their tradition was continued by V. Zítek, O. Horáková, J. Novotná, M. Krásová (who sang the role of Smetana's Libuše for many years), M. Podvalová, Z. Otava and B. Blachut; and more recently by V. Přibyl, P. Dvorský, V. Soukupová and G. Beňačková. Most of these artists have achieved international celebrity and it is therefore not surprising that Czechoslovak opera ensembles have traditionally attracted great interest throughout the world. They have performed in the Soviet Union, the Federal Republic of Germany, the Netherlands, Spain and Italy, etc.

Czechoslovak ballet also has a tradition of excellence which continues today. The work of the first artists, represented between the two world wars by A. Berger, J. Jenčík and S. Machov, and after the Second World War by M. Kůra, has been continued by, for example, M. Drottnerová, V. Harapes, J. Němeček, P. Šmok and M. Pesiková. The success of the Czech ballet school is also demonstrated by the appreciation shown our dancers at international competitions in countries such as Japan and the United States.

Pantomime occupies an outstanding place in Czechoslovak stage life. L. Fialka is one of the leading mime artists of the world, and there is also the Black Theatre (headed by J. Srnec) and the Theatre of Leading-strings (headed by B. Polívka). The Czechoslovak pantomime theatres are well known and have taken part in many international festivals, winning several important awards. On the borderline between stage and film art, the Magic Lantern, even after twenty-five years of existence, continues to attract audiences from Prague as well as spectators from abroad.

Czechoslovak stage design is of a high standard and has developed from the pre-war traditions symbolized by names such as V. Hofman, F. Muzika, M. Kouřil and F. Tröster. Contemporary designers such as J. Svoboda, L. Vychodil, K. Dudič, Z. Kolár, D. Gálik, M. Pokorný, J. Sládek and others are widely known. The Prague Quadriennales are exhibitions of stage art. They are highlights of Czechoslovak cultural life and an occasion to exchange international experiences.

Czech and Slovak puppetry has a unique position in the country and throughout the world. It has a long tradition, going back to the national revival, and is represented in Bohemia by M. Kopecký and in Slovakia by J. Stražan. In addition to important professional puppet theatres (Spejbl and Hurvínek Theatre, Central Puppet Theatre, The Dragon, etc.) there are also many amateur ensembles, for which different festivals and competitions are organized every year. Czech and Slovak puppets have successfully penetrated the film studios, and millions of children and adults have enjoyed them. The puppet films and animated cartoons by J. Trnka, H. Týrlová, B. Pojar, K. Zeman, J. Brdečka, Z. Miler and others have succeeded thanks to their original scripts, their poetic character and their wit.

### The visual arts

The Czech and Slovak visual arts have a heritage stretching from the Gothic period to the nineteenth century. Mention has been made of medieval painting and architecture, the painters and sculptors of the time of Rudolph II and of the Baroque era. The founders of modern Czech painting are F. Tkadlík (whose work still shows the older classical feeling, although as a teacher at the Prague Academy of Art he taught the new generation of romantics) and particularly A. Mánes, who first laid the foundations of Czech landscape painting. The romanticists J. Mánes and A. Kosárek, the realists J. Navrátil, K. Purkyně and S. Pinkas, and a little later the group who worked on the pictorial decoration of the National Theatre in Prague (M. Aleš, V. Hynais, F. Ženíšek) all reassessed their work. On the borderline between realism and the new vision was A. Slavíček, the country's most important impressionist, and following him the first representatives of modern painting emerged. First, there was the group of decorative-style artists, the best-known being Alfons Mucha, designer of the famous posters of Sarah Bernhardt, F. Kupka, one of the

23

first abstract painters, J. Preisler and V. Preissig. R. Kremlička was influenced by expressionism; B. Kubišta, E. Filla, V. Špála and J. Čapek adopted cubism; the representatives of surrealism were notably Toyen, J. Štyrský and J. Šíma, and of kineticism, Z. Pešánek. J. Zrzavý and F. Tichý are noted for their individual style. L. Fulla and M. Benka were inspired by Slovak folklore and landscape.

Post-war and contemporary painting is represented by a number of artists, such as J. Bauch, J. Grus, F. Jiroudek, K. Souček, O. Dubay, J. Želibský, A. Pelc, V. Rabas, K. Svolinský, V. Rada, W. Nowak, V. Beneš, K. Lhoták, J. Liesler, C. Bouda, J. Mudroch, R. Koldř, C. Majernik, M. Medvecká, V. Hložnik and A. Brunovsky. Czech and Slovak painters have successfully exhibited abroad. Czechoslovak graphic art (by, among others, J. Švengsbír, J. Anderle and V. Suchánek) is also well known abroad, as are the book illustrations by artists, such as J. Lada, L. Jiřincová, O. Janeček, M. Troup, Z. Burian, A. Born, and so on. Their work, particularly that for children's books, shows an understanding of the child's receptivity and sensibility. Czech and Slovak cartoonists publish their work in satirical magazines, such as *Dikobraz* and *Rohac*, as well as holding individual exhibitions which attract great attention.

Czech and Slovak sculpture, after the Gothic and Baroque periods, reappeared again only towards the end of the nineteenth century, first in the work of J. V. Myslbek, who was spiritually connected with the revival, but also showed a strong sympathy with antiquity as well as with contemporary French sculpture. His synthesis of romanticism and monumental realism originated thus, and the impact of it influenced the work of some representatives of later generations. Already, at that time, the new decorative style appeared (Jugendstil), in the work of L. Šaloun, impressionism in the work of J. Mařatka and J. Štursa, together with F. Bílek's symbolism and O. Guttfreund's cubism. The next generation produced outstanding personalities such as V. Makovský, B. Kafka, K. Pokorný, R. Pribiš, J. Kulich, F. Štefunek, J. Kostka, B. Stefan, J. Lauda, K. Dvořák, K. Lidický, J. Malejovsky, J. Hdua, J. Simota and others.

Czech architecture, having produced in the nineteenth century brilliant works by J. Zítek and having expressed the ideals of the neo-Renaissance in a deeply national spirit (the most important buildings by Zítek are the National Theatre in Prague, the Rudolfinum—House of Artists, the Mill Colonnade in Karlovy Vary), at the turn of the century went through a revolutionary development connected with the ideas in the visual arts at that time. J. Kotěra, J. Gočár, F. Kysela and P. Janák are among the architects of the most important buildings of the Jugendstil period, and also of the later cubist period, when new names also appeared, such as V. Hoffman, designer of excellent interiors, J. Chochol and J. Kroha. In the functionalist period, J. Krejcar, J. Havlíček, K. Honzík and B. Fuks excelled. The ideas of these pioneers of modern architecture were taken up by later generations who were able, in the different conditions afforded by the socialist principles of construction, to develop fully the architecture which corresponded to the urgent needs of the time.

The building of new housing, health and cultural facilities, sports complexes, business centres, etc., demonstrates the possibilities offered by socialism for the aesthetic incorporation of new buildings into the built-up areas of the town and the natural environment. R. Podzemný, A. Tencer, R. Pastor, M. Marcinka, D. Kuzma, E. Kramár, I. Matušík, K. Prager, J. Polák, F. Cubr, K. Hubáček and V. Machonin are some of the representatives of this generation of contemporary Czech and Slovak architects.

Architectural activity in Czechoslovakia is also to be seen in the restoration of historical monuments, in which prominent architects participate. Prague Castle and other important historical buildings, not only in Prague and Bratislava, but throughout the country, are systematically restored. The State Institute for the Reconstruction of Town Reserves and Historical Monuments plays an important role in this work.

A significant role in the field of Czechoslovak visual arts is played by the *applied arts*. The glass industry began as early as the seventeenth century with the production of Bohemian crystal. At present, in addition to this traditional glass, metallurgical glass, cut and ground glass are widely produced. Among the many designers of glass, mention must be made of L. Smrčková and S. Libenský. Czech jewellery is also well known, particularly for its garnets. Today, in addition to the classic materials, unusual materials are used to emphasize the artistic and unique character of the work. Ceramic production has also achieved numerous international successes; prominent designers being O. Eckert, J. Radová and M. Taberyová.

Tapestry is a more recent but nevertheless fruitful art form, the beginnings of which are connected with M. Teinibzerová. It can be based either on an original design (A. Kybal) or on the adaptation of painters' works into tapestries as, for example, in the work of C. Bouda. The most recent types of textile production are closely linked with tapestry—the so-called art protis and lace tapestry inspired either by folklore or adopting modern means of expression.

Even at the beginning of the twentieth century, some prominent artists (J. Horejs, V. Špála, etc.) realized the importance of toys in positively influencing the development and education of children. Today this branch of applied art is fully recognized, and a number of Czechoslovak toys have achieved international success.

Czech artists achieved considerable success in typography in the period between the two world wars (K. Dyrynk, O. Menhart, M. Kaláb). However, at that time their work was limited, due to the small number of copies of books printed for a rather narrow circle of readers and bibliophiles.

Typography was only able to increase its social influence in the period of the socialist cultural development, when a high level of 'book culture' became an important aspect of publishers' activities.

Posters have a wide impact on daily life and have gained numerous awards at international competitions. Besides their publicity function, they also encourage the protection of health and of the environment as well as the struggle for peace.

One of the originators of the smallest branch of the applied arts, the production of postage stamps, was an outstanding artist, Alfons Mucha. This helped to stimulate further development and, as a result, the designers of contemporary stamps are prominent painters and engravers. The abundance of themes depicted and the quality of printing have made Czechoslovak stamps much sought after by philatelists.

## Music

Music has always been an important part of the national culture. Church music developed in the ninth century and secular music in the thirteenth, beginning under the influence of the *minnesingers*. In the fifteenth century, the most significant development was the Hussite chorales. In Slovakia, polyphony (the Kosice graduals) developed, and this form was represented in Bohemia, in particular by Kryštof Harant z Polžic. In Baroque music, a specific Czech style was created, influenced by domestic folk art. The music of A. V. Michna z Otradovic, B. M. Černohorský, the musical pedagogue and composer, J. Třenovský and J. Francisci is still widely played. F. X. Brixi wrote a number of ecclesiastical compositions and piano sonatas, and J. K. Vaňhal composed 100 symphonies, 100 quartets and 23 masses. He was surpassed by J. J. Ryba, composer of almost 1,500 works, the most famous of them being the Czech Christmas Mass, a musical jewel whose outer spiritual framework contains elements of folk music and literary traditions.

From the eighteenth century, Czech musicians became known abroad, for example in the so-called Mannheim School, whose main representative and founder was J. V. Stamic. This school created a new instrumental style, and in developing the sonata and symphonic forms anticipated the further evolution of classical music. Countless Czech composers and musical pedagogues worked abroad and influenced European music, among them J. Mysliveček and Bedřich Smetana, who was for a certain time a conductor at Gothenburg, Sweden. His work laid the foundations of modern Czech music, especially opera. No less famous is his cycle of symphonic poems, *My Country*, and the quartet, *From My Life*.

His work was continued by Antonin Dvořák, composer of the *New World Symphony* and the *Slavonic Dances*, and by Zdeněk Fibich who created a new musical genre in his trilogy *Hippodamia* —the melodrama. Due to the originality of his musical ideas it was L. Janáček who first became world famous. The national musical tradition continued to develop in the works of V. Novák, J. Suk, J. B. Foerster, A. Moyzes, J. Cikker, the founder of the Slovak opera, E. Suchoň, O. Jeremiáš, A. Hába, B. Martinů and other composers.

Contemporary Czechoslovak music is significant for its wide range of content and form. It is to be found in the regular repertoire of conductors throughout the world, and new works are presented to the public during special weeks which are organized every year in Czechoslovakia. Among contemporary composers, mention should be made of P. Eben, L. Zeleany, S. Havelka and O. Flosman. In the post-war period, there have been notable developments in the composition of cantatas and songs, especially those of J. Seidl and V. Dolia. V. V. Trojan's music constitutes an integral part of the puppet films of J. Trinka.

An inseparable aspect of Czechoslovak musical culture is the art of its presentation. Among the older generation, the best-known representatives were J. Kubelík, O. Ševčik and F. Ondříček, and among the contemporaries mention should be made of J. Suk, J. Páleníček and J. Ropek.

As the distinguished Director of the Opera of the National Theatre of Prague and Conductor of the Czech Philharmonic Orchestra, V. Talich had a long career. Among conductors, we must also mention Z. Chalabala, L. Rajter, J. Krombholz and K. Ančerl. The Czech Philharmonic Orchestra is directed today by V. Neumann and the Slovak Philharmonic Orchestra by L. Slovák. The famous Czech quartets are engaged by a whole series of concert organizations together with artists who are still very young. Among the most prominent are the Smetana Quartet, the Suk Quartet, the Talich Quartet, the Janáček Quartet, the Panocha Quartet, the Suk Trio and the Czech Nonet.

In Czech and Slovak musical life an important part is played by professional and amateur choirs, which are having considerable success at music festivals abroad. While Czech and Slovak concert artists represent their country all over the world (in the last few years they could be heard at more than seventy musical festivals, and of the twenty symphony orchestras that exist in Czechoslovakia, seventeen performed abroad), our cultural life is being enriched by the visits of leading world concert artists. In Czechoslovakia, every year four big music festivals are organized, the best-known being the Prague Spring and the Bratislava Musical Festivities (See Table 2).

The high level of Czech and Slovak musical life is demonstrated not only by concerts but also by recordings. Records are sold in Czechoslovakia of all the important works of world music performed by leading national and foreign concert artists, and the Artia Publishing House exports every year 200,000 records of all types, but mainly classical music. Thus, the works of important Czech and Slovak classic composers are promoted,

27

TABLE 2.                     State musical ensembles in Czechoslovakia, 1955–82

| Year | Number of ensembles | Number of concerts | Number of visitors (1,000s) | Number of visitors: index = 100 |
|------|------|------|------|------|
| 1955 | 17 | 1 444 | 992 | 100.00 |
| 1960 | 17 | 3 491 | 2 264 | 228.20 |
| 1965 | 18 | 4 178 | 2 278 | 229.60 |
| 1970 | 22 | 3 553 | 2 076 | 209.20 |
| 1975 | 22 | 3 588 | 2 459 | 247.90 |
| 1980 | 23 | 3 503 | 1 830 | 184.40 |
| 1981 | 24 | 3 757 | 1 969 | 188.40 |
| 1982 | 23 | 4 311 | 2 023 | 203.90 |

particularly, by the records of the series 'Musica Antiqua Bohemica' and 'Musica Nova Bohemica'. Extraordinary success has been achieved abroad by the complete recordings of Beethoven's and Mahler's symphonies and the complete editions of the works of Smetana, Dvořák and Janáček. The quality of exported gramophone records is demonstrated also by more than fifty prizes at international festivals, among others the prize of the Italian gramophone critics, several Grands Prix du Disque of the Académie Charles Cros as well as the Grand Prix of the French Academy.

# Cultural policy

## Principles and legal norms

Czechoslovak cultural policy is based on the profound cultural traditions of the Czech and Slovak nations and guarantees that the targets of the socialist cultural revolution are met. This revolution is the transformation of man's life-style and consciousness, in order to ensure progressive individual and social development. The practical implementation of the cultural and educational function of the state consists of ensuring the personal, economic, material, technical and legislative conditions for the development of the system of cultural and social institutions and of the cultural life of the population.

The cultural policy programme of Czechoslovakia is based on several main principles.

First, there is the *principle of the democratization of culture*, the consistent implementation of which is typical of Czechoslovak cultural policy and which is the basic prerequisite for cultural development in our society. Democratization of culture aims to create institutional conditions which will enable all members of society to have access to the cultural values of the past and present and to be prepared according to their cultural level and education to relate positively to these values. It is characteristic of socialist democratization of culture that in addition to professional artists and creators, amateur artists also participate in the establishment of cultural values. Facilities are available on a nationwide scale to enable them to implement their creative and artistic interests, to develop their talents and thus contribute to the development of national culture and art.

The political structure of Czechoslovakia is based on the principle of democratic centralism, which is also the principle for the implementation of cultural policy. Its aim is to ensure that not only the creators of cultural values, but also their consumers participate in cultural policy and that it is implemented at all levels, from the Federal Assembly, through the

29

Czech and Slovak National Councils, to the National Committees. These representative organs of the people have cultural commissions whose members are elected from among the voters of the respective territorial units which ensure the active participation of citizens in the administration of culture at the national level. Broad democratic participation in administration is ensured by membership of the people's and special interest organizations in the National Front, an organization representative of all the component parts of our society.

The *principle of socialist humanism and internationalism* is implemented in two basic ways. The Czech and Slovak cultures have always developed, in the course of their history of more than one thousand years, in the context of European and world culture and art, from which they have taken progressive cultural and artistic values while at the same time contributing in different historical periods and art forms to their enrichment. At present, progressive works of art in the fields of drama, cinema, literature, television, music, the graphic and plastic arts, etc., are being imported on a large scale. The second method of implementing the principle of internationalism is to propagate abroad the important values of Czech and Slovak artistic production and the art of our performers, thus contributing to world culture.

The *principle of popularization* is typical of the Czech and Slovak cultures at all stages of their development. The democratic and popular character of our art and culture is borne out by the fact that our artistic creators, like our scientific workers, come from the roots of the people, and their efforts have been directed to serving the current and prospective needs of the masses, not those of a restricted élite class. The principle of popularization implies, in the first place, the need for intelligibility whilst maintaining exacting standards on the artistic and ideological levels. The condition for implementing this principle is educating citizens to appreciate works of culture and art. This is taken care of by the education system at all levels.

The *principle of the scientific approach* is an inevitable condition of the conception and implementation of the cultural policy and its projections into medium-term plans as well as into the long-term development of Czech and Slovak cultures. In addition to this fundamental conceptual role, scientific research contributes to the understanding of the cultural life of individual groups within our society and to its development.

The implementation of the socialist cultural policy is ensured by the *system of legal norms*, i.e. in the first place by the Constitution of the Czechoslovak Socialist Republic, by individual acts and by other legislative acts.

The Czechoslovak state had already legally regulated some sectors of cultural activity before the Second World War. At the beginning of the 1920s there was the promulgation of the act on municipal libraries, on educational courses for the people and on municipal records. However, these partial legal provisions did not cover the whole field of culture.

In the first months after the liberation of Czechoslovakia from Nazi occupation, the Decree on state and cultural educational care was promulgated, which represented some progress in the conception of the cultural function of the state and ensured the possibility of its implementation. Also at that time the Decree on the nationalization of the film industry which eliminated commercial viewpoints from the cinema was promulgated and facilitated, its extensive development demonstrated by outstanding international successes.

A distinct transformation took place after 1948 with the gradual promulgation of Acts ensuring further democratic cultural development of society. The unifying principle of all these Acts is stated in the Constitution of the Czechoslovak Socialist Republic where we read:

The state, together with the people's organizations, shall give all possible support to creative activity in science and art, shall endeavour to achieve an increasingly high educational level of the working people and their active participation in scientific and artistic work, and shall see to it that the results of this work serve all the people.

From among the most important Acts, mention should be made of those on theatres, educational and cultural activity, cultural monuments, state protection of nature, popular artistic production, museums and galleries, the uniform system of libraries, national artists and copyright. The above-mentioned acts define individual spheres of culture, specify the tasks of the state in ensuring their development and form the basis of the institutional and material guarantees of Czechoslovak culture.

## Organizational structure
## of individual branches of culture

To safeguard the cultural process, there is in Czechoslovakia, as in other countries, an independent system, from the state organizations down to voluntary leisure-time organizations.

The supreme organ is the Federal Assembly with overall legislative authority. This body, which solves the fundamental state-wide problems concerning the life of nations, as well as of ethnic groups, in the Czechoslovak Socialist Republic, concerns itself also with the basic questions of cultural life. In the first place, it discusses all Acts concerning the cultural development of society and controls their observation. It also approves government programmes, including their cultural and political aspects, and every year discusses the respective cultural chapter in the report of the government. To facilitate the work of the government and its ministries, working commissions from among the deputies are set up specializing in the problems of different fields. Questions connected with cultural development are solved in the Federal Assembly by the Cultural Commission, which discusses them with members of the government and important cultural representatives.

Because the Czechoslovak Socialist Republic is a federation of two national republics, the Federal Assembly has a legislative body in the Czech Socialist Republic and another in the Slovak Socialist Republic. The supreme legislative organs of the two republics are the Czech National Council and the Slovak National Council. All questions concerning the cultural development of both republics are discussed and resolved by the Cultural and Educational Committees of these councils, together with their plenary sessions and presidiums.

There are two Ministries of Culture, one in the Czech Socialist Republic and one in the Slovak Socialist Republic. They are headed by the Ministers of Culture of both national governments as constitutional functionaries, and they co-ordinate their work through direct operative co-operation, and also through regular co-ordinating consultative meetings at the level of the governing bodies of both ministries. Problems of state-wide significance are solved through co-ordination, particularly concerning the preparation of individual acts, the unification of regulations, economic questions and the negotiation of a uniform procedure in the field of foreign cultural relations, the representation of the country in international organizations, etc.

In the Federal Government, it is the Deputy Prime Minister who deals with culture at this level, as well as looking after some other departments in the non-productive sphere.

In the Czechoslovak system of state administration, *decentralization in the form of a system of national committees* is implemented according to the principle of democratic centralism. This system comprises, in descending order, the Regional, District and Local National Committees. The national committees develop their activity on the basis of the Act concerning them. They are elected bodies with executive authority within their field of competence and, as such, they consist of the plenum and the council and are headed by a chairman. For important fields of activity, the national committees set up specialized commissions from among their members, including cultural commissions. The national committees co-operate closely with the civil committees (non-state organs composed of voters from the local ward.) The administrative work of the national committees is assured by their professional structure.

The main burden of state administration rests on the national committees. In the cultural sphere, they prepare, on the basis of their electoral programme, the plan for the cultural development of their province; in accordance with the state plan and by means of the state cultural policy they are responsible, within the province, for the activity of cultural organizations. The national committees are responsible for cinemas, club facilities, local as well as people's libraries, local museums, observatories, parks for culture and recreation, zoos and historical and cultural monuments

Jitřenka (Morning Star) children's folklore ensemble at Český Krumlov. A rehearsal.

The Jiří Trnka Studio for puppet films in Prague.

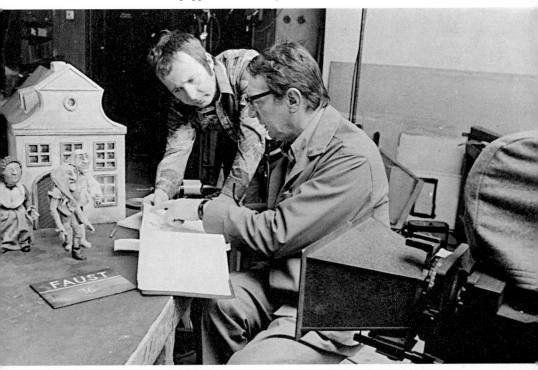

Conservation of the cultural heritage at Roztoky near Prague. Irradiation of objects.

The Na Zábradlí (On the Railings) Theatre in Prague. Ladislav Fialka Pantomime.

of local significance. The District National Committees control the district people's libraries, district museums and more important cultural monuments. The Regional National Committees are responsible for theatres, scientific libraries, national parks and nature reserves, symphony orchestras, historical and cultural monuments of national significance and regional museums.

The Regional National Committees are answerable to the government, and their cultural activity is directed by the national Ministries of Culture. The forms of this management are laid down by law and are implemented, to a considerable extent, through legislative measures—instructions, different forms of co-operation and professional management, and the working sessions of the corresponding senior officials of the Regional National Committees and of the Ministries of Culture.

With regard to the national Ministries of Culture which are the central bodies of state administration in the sphere of culture, there are certain differences in organizational structure and range of activities resulting from differences in conditions in the two national republics, due to their historical development. In principle, however, the ministries are equal partners with corresponding spheres of action. Individual bodies of the ministries under the state administration have central control over the following fields:

*Art and literature* (theatres, concert activities, painting, sculpture, graphic art, applied art, book publishing, music publishing, including the production of gramophone records and cassettes, agency activity).

*Cultural and educational activities* (particularly club activities and hobbies, amateur art activities, museology, librarianship, galleries, specialized cultural facilities such as observatories, zoos, parks for culture and recreation, etc.).

*The conservation of historical and cultural monuments and the protection of nature* (historical collections and architectural monuments as part of the cultural heritage of historical or artistic value, nature reserves—protected territories and protected natural monuments).

*International cultural relations* (carried out at state level).

In addition, the ministries have a number of activities of an auxiliary character. There is extensive planning which includes the long-term, medium-term and annual operational plans of all state cultural organizations, registration of plan fulfilment, the system of socio-economic unformation (statistics) and the automated systems for collection and elaboration of information.

Long-term planning and management of the complicated system of cultural sections and institutions requires the co-operation of research institutions. The Ministries of Culture have at their disposal a number of such departmental institutions in the field of social sciences and also in science and technology. In Prague there are, for example, the Institute for Research in Culture, the Institute for Cultural and Educational Activity, the Theatre Institute, the Institute for Information and Management, the Research Institute of Sound, Picture and Reproductive Technology. In Bratislava, there are the Research Institute of Culture, the Institute for Adult Education, etc. All these research facilities form the basis of departmental research, together with the centrally planned and administered activities. Within its terms of reference, the department participates also in the solution of individual research problems connected with the State Plan for the Development of Science and Technology, and in some cases it also takes part in internationally co-ordinated research tasks.

The Ministries of Culture rely on their technical and economic bodies to ensure the conditions for the implementation of cultural programmes. They solve the problems of financing, technological development, manpower, investments, etc. Of no lesser importance are the professional training of cultural workers and legislative activity.

In addition to their professional and functional bodies, the ministries have advisory organs, constituted either on the basis of existing regulations or by the decision of ministers. They have a professional or scientific character and can be subdivided into those answerable to *ministers* and those answerable to *ministries*. The advisory organs of ministers consult with the governing body of the Ministry and Minister's Council. In addition, the ministers are responsible for the activity of such advisory organs as the Board for Questions on Cultural Funds, the Scientific Council and the Central Councils for Librarianship, for Cultural and Educational Activity, for State Conservation of Historical and Cultural Monuments, for Museums and Galleries, etc. Apart from these advisory organs directed by ministers, most bodies in the ministries have a number of auxiliary advisory organs whose activity is focused on special sectors, as for example: the Theatre Council, the Council for Symphony Orchestras, the Co-ordinating Council of the Gramophone Section, the Advisory Board for the Parks for Culture and Recreation, the Advisory Board for the Publishing of Literature for Children and Youth, the Committee for the Social Sciences, the Committee for Technical Sciences, etc.

The majority of cultural institutions come within the domain of the national committees but there are a number of organizations administered directly by the ministries. In the first place, there are the organizations whose activity covers the whole territory of individual republics or is of national importance, such as, for example, prominent theatres, state philharmonic orchestras, central museums, central galleries, central studios for the restoration of works of art and organizations which produce cultural goods, particularly establishments turning out records and cassettes, or manufacturing technological equipment for theatres, engineering works for cultural facilities, specialized establishments which set up exhibitions at home and abroad, organizations for arts and crafts, folk crafts, etc. Among the centrally administered organizations, agencies organizing the engagements of performers at home and abroad or representing writers and playwrights are also included. Specialized and research institutions of a theoretical or professional and methodological nature are centrally administered by the ministries.

In addition to the organizations administered directly by the ministries, there exist within the same framework independent organizations whose establishment was based upon an independent legislative act. First, there are the Czech and Slovak *Cultural Funds*, namely literary funds (including also individual branches of dramatic art), music funds and art funds. There are also the unions representing artists' copyright in Czechoslovakia and abroad.

It is necessary to go into more detail concerning the complicated and important role of these funds in the cultural life of Czechoslovakia. Their broad programme of social security for artists is implemented in the form of scholarships for creative activity, study abroad, creative assistance for young emerging artists, interest-free advances and loans, and the activity of specific establishments (publishing houses, music publishing houses, negotiators of the purchase and sale of works of art, centres for recreational, working or curative stays, etc.). It is financed by the 3 per cent contribution fee from artists' royalties and, at the same time, by the money resulting from the decision by which the Czechoslovak state renounced its income from copyright and used it to credit these funds. The funds are also used to provide artists with social security in the form of an obligatory health and old-age insurance, in the case of freelance artists, and of voluntary insurance when the artists are wage-earners who, in connection with their part-time artistic activity, wish to improve their insurance benefits. There are thousands of cultural workers who benefit from these provisions, which cover all the artistic and specialized professions, including writers, composers, painters, actors, theoreticians, critics, publicists, stage directors, screen-writers, cameramen, announcers and industrial designers.

These funds have their own publishing houses. The Music Fund has a publishing house for records and the Art Fund has a network of its own art galleries. In this way, the funds disseminate their members' productions on a wide scale.

A special position is held by the *Creative Art Unions* which exist on the basis of the Act on Voluntary Organizations and the *State-wide (Federal) Organizations of Film, Radio and Television*. The mass media work mostly outside the direct province of the Ministries of Culture.

However, there are also a number of organizations dealing with culture which are not within the sphere of culture, as specified in the methodology of the state plan. The commercial organization, Artcentrum, operates within the Department of the Federal Ministry of Foreign Trade. Besides exporting cultural goods, it is also responsible for the protection of artists' copyright. Other departments are concerned with cultural activity. For example, in the armed forces there exists a whole range of cultural activities with amateur as well as professional ensembles, publishing houses, periodicals, film production, etc.

An other important role in centralized cultural life, as well as in that of individual regions, is played by the *non-state organizations*. First, there are the political, cultural and educational activities carried out by political organizations, associated in the National Front. All the political parties have their own press, their own publishing houses and their own cultural programmes. The most important is, of course, the activity of the largest component of the National Front, the *Revolutionary Trade Union Movement*. This organization of many millions of members, bringing together in its trade unions employees from all spheres and branches, has its own network of clubs, libraries and other cultural and recreational facilities. All the employers' organizations make contributions to the fund for cultural and social needs jointly with the trade unions, and among other activities they finance the collective participation of the employees in different cultural events. In a similar way, the *co-operative organizations* participate in the cultural life of society; and here, of course, they fulfil the cultural functions not provided by the trade union organs. Another non-state institution is the *Socialist Union of Youth* with its own press, publishing houses and a network of youth clubs as well as other facilities (for example, its own travel agency). Other institutions associated with the National Front are also engaged in cultural activity. The *Socialist Academy* and the *Czechoslovak Scientific and Technological Society* have a specific cultural mission. These organizations mostly bring together cultural and scientific workers for voluntary cultural, educational and popular scientific work.

As they are trade-unionists, workers in the cultural sector are organized within the framework of the Revolutionary Trade Union Movement in an independent *Trade Union of the Workers of Art, Culture and Social Organizations*. This trade union assures its members extensive social care, legal protection and recreation in Czechoslovakia and abroad.

## Financing individual cultural activities

In view of the importance attached to cultural development in Czechoslovakia, its economic aspect is taken care of by state and social institutions. In principle, most sums spent on financing cultural and artistic activities in Czechoslovakia are covered from social sources. In the first place, funds come from the state budget (see Table 3), which provides in individual independent chapters for the financial settlement of the operational and investment activity of all cultural organizations within the province of the Ministries of Culture and Films, Radio and Television (see Table 4). The funds for the organizations that come within the domain of the national committees are included in the budgets of the Regional National Committees which redistribute them as needed. Further funds are transferred

TABLE 3. State budget expenditures and social consumption, 1978–80 (in millions of Kčs at current prices)

|  | 1978 | 1979 | 1980 |
|---|---|---|---|
| *State expenditure* | | | |
| Expenditure of the state budget and of the budgets of the National Committees | 283 912 | 292 403 | 304 182 |
| Expenditure on culture | 4 895 | 5 300 | 5 792 |
| Expenditure on culture as a percentage of the total expenditures from the state budget and from the budgets of the National Committees | 1.72 | 1.81 | 1.90 |
| Index of the growth of expenditure on culture | 100.00 | 108.30 | 118.30 |
| *Social consumption* | | | |
| Total social consumption | 136 998 | 141 391 | 151 245 |
| Social consumption on culture | 5 773 | 6 013 | 6 067 |
| Social consumption on culture as a percentage of total social consumption | 4.21 | 4.25 | 4.01 |

*Source:* Statistical yearbooks of the Czechoslovak Socialist Republic.
*Note:* Expenditure on culture (from the State Budget and within the framework of the social consumption) is *mostly expenditure on cultural services* (most objects of a cultural character purchased in the retail network are covered from the population's personal incomes).

TABLE 4. State expenditure supplements supporting theatre, cinema and concert attendance, 1978–80

|  | 1978 | 1979 | 1980 |
|---|---|---|---|
| *Theatres* | | | |
| Additional supplement by the state per visitor in Kčs | 56.67 | 60.52 | 61.24 |
| Percentage of the additional supplement by the state to the expenditures per visitor | 83.03 | 83.87 | 83.81 |
| Percentage of the admission fee of the expenditures per visitor | 16.97 | 16.13 | 16.19 |
| *Cinemas* | | | |
| Additional supplement by the state per visitor in Kčs | 1.72 | 1.01 | 1.34 |
| Percentage of the additional supplement by the state to the expenditures per visitor | 13.40 | 8.01 | 9.80 |
| Percentage of the admission fee of the expenditures per visitor | 86.60 | 91.98 | 90.20 |
| *Music* | | | |
| Additional supplement by the state per visitor in Kčs | 77.54 | 87.30 | 72.62 |
| Percentage of the additional supplement by the state to the expenditures per visitor | 92.45 | 93.30 | 90.08 |
| Percentage of the admission fee of the expenditures per visitor | 7.55 | 6.70 | 9.92 |

*Source:* Statistical yearbooks of culture of the Czechoslovak Socialist Republic.

to the field of culture from the budgets of other departments which participate within their province in cultural development. Funds are also transferred from the social organizations and, in the first place, from the employers' organizations which, together with the trade unions, share the so-called 'Funds of Cultural and Social Needs'. It is also necessary to mention the amounts spent by users of establishments which come under the conservation of historical and cultural monuments for their upkeep. This is approximately four to five times the sum allocated from the state budget. The total amount approaches 1 billion korunas.

As regards methods of financing, there are three basic types of organization. The *economic organizations* are mostly of a productive or commercial type and cover their operating expenses and investment activity from their own income before giving the profit to the state budget. There are not many economic organizations in the cultural sector of the Czechoslovak Socialist Republic, and as a percentage of the total number of organizations of culture they fluctuated around 5 per cent in the last few years. Their income represented around 80 per cent of their total expenditure. Their economic independence is only relative, because profit for them is not decisive, only indicative. Organizations do not necessarily have to surrender their total profit, but can keep a part of it to cover expenses incurred in their work. If they surrender the total profit, this is used to serve cultural needs. For example, it might be used to assist organizations which are of the contributory type.

The *contributory organizations* are run on a state allocation, and form about 67 per cent of the total number of cultural organizations. When such an organization has its own income, this comes mostly from admission fees. This is the case for theatres, museums, galleries, etc., i.e. institutions in the field of cultural services. This income represents about 50 per cent of the amount necessary to cover operational and investment costs. In its plan, the organization first specifies the amount of its own income and the amount of the state allocation. Any additional sums that the organization earns through its work may be used under specific conditions to enlarge its activities and strengthen its funds.

Lastly, there are the *budgetary organizations*. They operate on a budget which is covered fully by the state allocation and, in this way, the higher authorities allocate funds in particular to research and scientific organizations, etc. There are organizations whose activities are non-profit-making or which, in the social interest, prefer not to employ a commercial approach. Their income is thus the lowest and represents around 15 per cent of the total expenditure. They form about 28 per cent of the total number of cultural organizations.

Cultural policy

**Financial sources**

The main sources of finance for cultural activities are the relevant items in the state budget (Federal Budget, Budgets of both republics and of the National Committees). Resources for culture are also drawn from the funds of industry and non-governmental organizations, in the first place trade unions, with the national committees and with industrial or agricultural concerns. Only a small proportion of the expenditure on culture is covered by the income from the cultural institutions themselves, obtained in the form of admission fees, payments for services, etc.

39

# Science on culture
# and for culture

Present-day problems of further cultural development in Czechoslovakia are being increasingly influenced by the scientific and technological revolution and by the fundamental transformation of the way of life in the process of building a developed socialist society. These social processes provide ways of overcoming theoretically and in practice the contradictions which may exist between civilization and culture, and also of reacting in a new way to cultural questions.

Contemporary research in culture is based on ancient and modern traditions which began to develop at the time of founding the Charles University. This university was for many years the centre of humanistic exploration of the cultural development of man and of work. As a result of the historical development of Bohemia, Moravia and Slovakia, interest in science was transferred during the eighteenth and nineteenth centuries, at the time of the national revival, to culture and to language as the source of national self-realization. In the twentieth century, individual disciplines of art criticism and history were intensively developed and, in some branches, research achieved remarkable results. At the same time, a new current came into existence aiming at a Marxist interpretation of the questions to be solved. However, this promising development was forcibly interrupted by the German occupation, when universities and all institutions of higher learning were closed, scientific and cultural institutions abolished, and the most prominent representatives of cultural and scientific life persecuted, many of them perishing in concentration camps.

The socialist state has made possible, by granting unprecedented financial, material and other resources, the fundamental reconstruction of the institutional and professional basis of scientific research. At present, there are 180,000 workers in the scientific and research field, 15,000 of whom are in the institutions of the Czechoslovak Academy of Sciences, whose foundation in 1952 helped to eliminate the dispersed and unco-ordinated character of fundamental research.

There was also development of research attached to individual Minis-tries, to the central organs of state administration and to some social organ-izations. Two departmental institutes devote themselves to direct research on culture—mainly the Research Institutes of Culture in Prague and in Bratislava. Some other institutions of the Ministries of Culture of the Czech Socialist Republic and of the Slovak Socialist Republic (the State Library of the Czech Socialist Republic, the Slovak Cultural Association—Matica, the Theatre Institute, the National Literature Museum, etc.), concern themselves with specialized questions of culture, as do the institutes of the Czechoslovak Academy of Sciences, a number of individual universities (particularly at the faculties of arts and research institutes attached to museums, art galleries, specialized libraries and archives). (For example, they deal with art, cultural and educational activity, cultural aspects of life-style, etc.) A Research Section in Radio, Television and Films has also been set up.

The most important tasks in the field of culture are to be found in the State Plan of the Development of Science and Technology, and this contributes to their interrelation and to a closer connection with cultural and social practice as well as to their introduction into broader international contexts. The results achieved are then assessed according to their relation to the present and prospective developmental needs of the society, the culture and the individual. The organs of management of the state admin-istration are responsible here for ensuring that the time span between the results of scientific knowledge and their application in cultural and social practice is minimal.

## Cultural research

Cultural research after liberation in 1945 evaluated and re-evaluated the results achieved before the war and solved the problems connected with the building of a socialist society. The basic questions of the democra-tization of culture, cultural and educational activity, aesthetic education and the function and mission of art were gradually analysed. The cultural dimension of the historical development of the Czech and Slovak nations, and questions of the specificity and processes of rapprochement between the Czech and Slovak cultures were analysed. The bases of the scientific management of culture were laid and ethnographic research was expanded. The development of research in the field of culture found, among other aspects, its practical expression in building up the network of cultural facilities and methodological centres for the organization of cultural life throughout the whole country.

Further efforts are being made at more comprehensive planning of cultural research and its close connection with social practice. The research is focused on the theory of art, the development of art and language, and aesthetic education, while research on general questions of culture concerns itself with shaping and satisfying the cultural needs and interests of the population, analysis of the development of folk culture in Bohemia, Moravia and Slovakia, material and technical conditions of the development of culture, the problems of leisure, life-style and questions of scientific management in the cultural field.

A notable turning-point in research came in the second half of the 1970s when the transition to qualitative exploration of the cultural component in human activity and to exploration of the role of culture in shaping the social consciousness took place. Other research during this period was directed at the cultural and social function of the mass media, the profile of the cultural and educational worker, the cultural life of workers and farmers, and at questions of the systematic protection and creation of the human environment. In addition to this research, which was essentially forward looking, the theory of culture was also developed. The result was the foundation of Departments of the Theory of Culture at the Faculties of Arts of individual universities in 1976.

At present, research on culture is focused on the analysis of basic cultural processes and their historical and socio-economic determinants. The sociology of culture concerns itself, in this connection, with problems of the cultural dimension of forming the personality, with the shaping, satisfaction and development of the cultural needs of the population, and with following qualitative changes in the culture of work and in the use of leisure.

In the field of art theory, the history of the arts and the linguistic field, the main tasks are, at present, the development of the theory of literature, the importance and role of the cultural heritage for cultural life in the socialist society, the fine arts and music of the twentieth century, Czech and Slovak as important bearers of the national culture, and comprehensive research into the question of artistic expression.

The general questions of socialist culture are mainly solved in the light of the characteristic features of its development, of the management of culture and of cultural policy. Considerable attention is paid here to the problems of integrating the traditions of folk culture into contemporary life, and developing aesthetic education and the cultural life of youth.

Scientific research in the field of museums and art galleries directs its programme towards the formation and interpretation of collections, stressing the aspect of classification and the presentation problems of exhibitions and of publications.

A project entitled 'The Stages of the Development of the Czechoslovak Socialist Culture and its Prognosis until 2000' deals with the great cultural dynamism of Czechoslovak society. Prospective activity, conceived in a comprehensive way as the pre-condition for raising the scientific level of management, overcomes partial approaches and expresses the dynamic conception of theoretical research in the field of culture. At present, and in the very near future, such activity is oriented to defining possibilities for further development of individual cultural fields and to the analysis of new or anticipated problems which could substantially influence cultural and social development.

# Cultural heritage

Czechoslovakia, as a country with a rich cultural past, has many historic art collections and architectural monuments which are an inseparable part of European culture. For the nations of Czechoslovakia, the cultural values which they represent are of extraordinary social importance because they strengthen awareness of the national identity. The conservation of historic monuments in Czechoslovakia has a long tradition. Today it is handled by the state through professional institutions—the State Institute for the Conservation of Historic and Cultural Monuments and for the Protection of Nature, and seventeen Regional Centres for the Conservation of Historic and Cultural Monuments and for the Protection of Nature.

In Czechoslovakia there are, in proportion to the geographical area and the size of the population, a high number of protected monuments. In all, 32,860 architectural sites and several hundred thousand items in art collections are registered as historic and cultural monuments. Their conservation covers a number of activities which can be divided into four basic sectors, namely: the protection of historic and cultural monuments and their organic integration into present developments; conservation and restoration; the professional administration of historic and cultural monuments; and the development of their cultural function. The planned conservation of cultural monuments also requires heavy expenditure which amounts every year to 1 billion korunas (0.5 per cent of the state budget).

## National cultural monuments

Individual historical and cultural monuments are divided into several categories. Those which constitute the most important part of the cultural heritage are declared by the government to be national cultural monuments, and at present there are 122 of them (78 of which are in Slovakia). The most important are Prague Castle and Bratislava Castle, followed by the

Czech coronation jewels, the Gothic Charles Bridge, built by Charles IV, with baroque statues, the compound of the Convent of the Blessed Agnes, founded by Agnes, daughter of Přemysl Otakar II, the Italian Courtyard in Kutná Hora, the site of the castle of the Přemyslids, Levý Hradec, the Říp Mountain with St George's Rotunda, Trocnov, the birthplace of Jan Žižka, the horse tramway from České Budějovice to Linz, and there are many others.

## Historic towns

Of great importance are the historic towns, which were mostly founded during the thirteenth and fourteenth centuries. The architectural and historical value of these towns depends on the extent and preservation of the original layout of the historic buildings and of the town fortifications. The most valuable town centres are declared historic town reserves. In Czechoslovakia, 1,200 have been preserved, out of which, the 45 most important are protected as historic reserves. Among the best known are Český Krumlov, Telč, Tábor, Písek, Prachatice, Slavonice, Čáslav, Cheb, Kremnica, Levoča, Kežmarok, Bardejov, Jihlava, České Budějovice and Banská Štianica.

In first place among the historic reserves is Prague, the capital of the Czechoslovak Socialist Republic. In a comparatively small area, 1,431 cultural monuments are concentrated, representing a whole range of European architectural styles. Pride of place belongs to Prague Castle, which for more than a thousand years has been the seat of the ruler of the Czech state and the focus of national history. This national cultural monument is the symbol of a famous past and thus the entire castle complex has been declared a protected area in the care of the Office of the President of the Republic. A firm place in history is also held by the Bethlehem Chapel in which Jan Hus used to preach, the Old Town Square, with the Old Town Hall, where important events took place during the Hussite period, the period after the Battle of the White Mountain and in modern times, and the National Theatre building which is the symbol of the national revival. Other no less famous cultural monuments are the second Prague castle of Vyšehrad, the oldest university building in Central Europe, the Carolinum, the New Town Hall, the National Museum, etc. Among the historic and cultural monuments some contemporary buildings, regarded as being most important from the artistic point of view, are also included. Their preservation for future generations is thus guaranteed.

## Architectural Monuments

Among the architectural monuments famous for their historical significance and artistic value, there are castles, chateaux, palaces, monasteries, churches and citadels. Out of a total of 3,000 castles and chateaux, about 200 which are considered the most important have been selected made and accessible to the public. The remainder are being restored or are in the care of the people's organizations. It was Karlštejn Castle, founded in 1348 by the King of Bohemia and the Holy Roman Emperor, Charles IV, which first became famous on a wider international scale. Its murals and paintings by Master Theodoricus are among the best specimens of fourteenth-century European art. The biggest castle in Central Europe is Spiš Castle in Slovakia. The Gothic Pernštejn Castle has been preserved since 1500, completely intact, due to its solid construction. Kost is one of the best preserved castles from the Luxemburg period and has a collection of Czech Gothic paintings and sculptures. The original Gothic castle of Jindřichův Hradec was rebuilt in the Renaissance style by Italian architects and contains examples of Czech Baroque, particularly work by Petr Brandl. The Humprecht Chateau is one of the most original buildings of the Czech Baroque, created by Carlo Lurago. The Queen Anna Summer Pavilion in Prague, built in the middle of the sixteenth century, is the most beautiful and the purest building in the Renaissance style north of the Alps.

Many ecclesiastical buildings are protected as historical monuments; they represent all styles from the Romanesque period to the present day, and are an integral part of the artistic heritage of our towns and villages. Today, the aesthetic and artistic function of these buildings is pre-eminent, and organ concerts are also organized in their impressive surroundings.

Architectural monuments and their interior furnishings form an historic ensemble. In their interior decoration, the aim is to preserve and/or restore the authentic state of the monuments as a whole. The organs for the conservation of historic monuments hold in some castles and chateaux exhibitions with a particular theme as, for example, in the Mikulov Chateau or in the small Kratochvíle Renaissance chateau. The extensive complexes of castles and palaces have parks and gardens; and architecture, sculpture and natural features have transformed them into works of art, as, for example, in the case of Veltrusy, Kroměříž, Lednice, Průhonice, etc., which fulfil an important aesthetic and educational function.

### Folk architecture

Czechoslovakia is very rich in folk architecture. In Central Europe there is no other country where, on such a small territory, there are so many types of folk building. They are evidence of creativeness and of an appreciation of the harmony of function, form and material integrated into a human environment. In Czechoslovakia three basic folk building areas are to be found. In the region of southern Slovakia and southern Moravia, there is the area of the earthen house; in the north-west, the half-timbered house is predominant, and in other areas, coming from the east, there is the log-house, which varies according to region (log-cottages with under-gables in the foothills of the Tatra Mountains and wooden houses in Moravian Wallachia), In these three areas there has more recently been a trend towards brick houses. A substantial number of the examples of folk architecture serve as permanent housing for a rural population and some of them as facilities for individual and group recreation. Valuable buildings that cannot be preserved in their original situation are moved to *skanzens* (Rožnov pod Radhoštěm, Zuberec, etc.).

## Historic collections

In addition to great architectural riches, the Czechoslovak Socialist Republic has also an inexhaustible quantity of important historic collections throughout its territory. The long tradition of collecting works of art goes back as far as the fourteenth century when Charles IV, at the time of the foundation of St Vitus's Cathedral in 1344, also began the collection which is now the church treasure. Although Charles's interest was directed, in the spirit of medieval piety, towards relics of saints, this very rich collection represents today a rare example of Czech and European craftsmanship from the tenth century onwards. A valuable collection of works of art was begun in Prague Castle at the end of the sixteenth century by the Emperor Rudolph II, and about a hundred years later, it was the Emperor Leopold I who resumed this work. Fragments of these collections, scattered in the course of the centuries as a result of war and other events, were restored in the 1960s and exhibited in the newly adapted rooms of the so-called New (Theresian) Palace in Prague Castle. The collections of the kings of Bohemia were continued by important noble families. Among the largest and oldest collections is that of Roudnice, which originated at the beginning of the seventeenth century. Today, a substantial part of it is installed in the chateau at Nelahozeves. It has, after Madrid and Vienna, the third largest collection of Spanish portraits, as well as ceramics from the middle of the sixteenth century onwards, a collection of goldsmiths' work from about 1600 etc. The State Office for the Conservation of Historic and Cultural Monuments preserves, restores and further increases these riches and tries to find for all collections a satisfactory home and method of exhibition.

The principal collection of art in Czechoslovakia is located in the National Gallery. This gallery is not situated in only one building, specially built or adapted for this purpose, but uses restored historic buildings in which complete collections of national and world art are presented. There is thus an interesting link between architectural monuments and art collections which enhances the effect of the paintings and sculptures. Czech art up to the eighteenth century is exhibited in St Georges' Monastery in Prague Castle (a former Benedictine monastery and the first on Czech territory, it was founded in the tenth century). Nineteenth-century

Czech painting is housed in the rooms of the former Convent of the Blessed Agnes in Prague (the Royal Poor Clares' Convent restored to its original thirteenth-century state) and European painting, particularly French art, is to be seen in the Šternberk Palace in Prague (an aristocratic palace dating from the beginning of the eighteenth century). Modern Czech sculpture is located in the former convent at Zbraslav, a suburb of Prague (the building dates from the beginning of the eighteenth century), and modern painting is exhibited in a palace dating from the 1920s.

In the Czechoslovak Socialist Republic, art collections are to be found not only in the capitals, but are also located in galleries and castles in all the regions (for example, the Moravian Bishops' Gallery in the Kroměříž Castle, the collection of South Bohemian Gothic sculpture in the newly adapted rooms of Hluboká Castle etc.).

Czechoslovakia is also rich in collections of the decorative and applied arts. In Prague, in addition to the permanent exhibition at the Museum of Arts and Crafts, there are two other world-famous collections of this type—the Loretto Santa Casa Treasure (with the famous diamond monstrance dating from 1699) and the Silver of the Czech Synagogues (part of the well-known State Jewish Museum). Mention should also be made of the museums containing unique discoveries on the territory of the former Great Moravian Empire (830–905). Such museums are to be found at Brno, in Staré Město u Uherského Hradiště, at Mikulčice, Nitra, etc. They are an example, among others, of the high standard of Czechoslovak archaeology.

In Czechoslovakia, there is a long-standing museums tradition. The National Museum Society was founded as early as 1818 and it was headed by the most important representatives of the national revival. The collections of the National Museum, housed in the building in Václavské Square in the centre of Prague, are constantly being enlarged in scope thanks to the care of the state, and have long since exceeded the limits imposed by a single building. To house some complete collections (examples of home culture and ethnographic collections from Asia, Africa and the Far East) different castles and palaces are being restored.

The historic collections are also rich in old manuscripts and incunabula. The state has inherited these treasures from various aristocratic and monastic collections, and continues to enlarge, preserve and restore them. They form the basis of the collections of the State Libraries of the Czech Socialist Republic and the Slovak Socialist Republic. Here, too, the principle has been followed of not harming the traditional collections by concentrating the most important books in one place. Thus one can find, in its original location, the well-known Strahov Library in the National Literature Museum in Prague (situated in the former Premonstratensian Monastery founded in 1142) with books from the tenth to eighteenth centuries, the library of the Vyšší Brod Monastery (founded in 1259) in South Bohemia, etc. In addition to its customary preservation of book

The Magic Lantern Theatre, Prague. From the performance of *The Magic Circus.*

The Palace of Culture, Prague.

International Master Summer School at the Academy of Musical Arts, Prague.

Baroque Theology Hall of the Strahov Monastery Library, Prague.

collections, the state spends large sums to produce facsimiles of old manu-scripts and incunabula in order to keep the originals of the most valuable books in air-conditioned safes, without affecting the complete collections.

## Social exploitation of cultural monuments

The conservationists strive not only to preserve and safeguard historic and cultural monuments, but also to integrate them into present-day life and provide new uses for them. Some historic buildings serve as housing. Some of the castles have been placed at the disposal of artistic and scien-tific institutions to provide a quiet environment for creative work. The remaining castles, provided they do not serve cultural and educational purposes directly as historic monuments, are utilized in a suitable way as seats of cultural institutions such as museums, galleries, archives and libraries. Schools, cultural and educational facilities, boarding-schools, old people's homes, health and social institutions have also been housed in them to advantage. The palaces, which are in the first place an integral part of the town layout, serve today mostly as the seats of offices or scientific and artistic institutions.

In the interior of a number of castles are modern installations for the exhibition of medieval ornamental sculpture and painting (Křivoklát, Kost), collections of old porcelain and earthenware (Loket). In some places, the castle interiors are evidence of collectors' tastes in the nineteenth century and for that reason they have been left intact (Hrádek u Nechanic, Hluboká, Orlík, Konopiště, Český Krumlov, etc.).

# Culture and nature

Czechoslovakia is a very varied country as regards natural resources. Its geological structure and its geographical location in the centre of Europe have encouraged a wealth of plant and animal communities. It is a country in which most Central European rivers have their source and three seas have their watershed. The weather is influenced from the west by the Atlantic, from the south by the Mediterranean, from the north by Scandinavia, and from the east by the continental climates. About 40,000 animal species and more than 2,500 plant species are to be found in Czechoslovakia. All the Central European types of landscape are to be seen, from plains and lowlands to hilly regions and mountain ridges. There are volcanic mountain ranges, river canyons, sandstone 'towns', limestone regions with caves and karst formations, steppes and forest steppes, peat-bogs, mineral sources, swamps, lakes, pond regions, meadows, woodland, etc.

## Tradition

The tradition of the protection of nature began to develop at the same time as in other countries. Among the oldest protected territories is the Žofínský Virgin Forest founded by the owner of the Nové Hrady Dominion in South Bohemia in 1838. The progressive attitude towards protection of nature in Czechoslovakia can be seen from examining the second-oldest protected territory, the Boubín Virgin Forest, preserved because of its scientific and research value since 1853. This forest reserve has been fully explored by contemporary researcher, continuing the scientific and research tradition of 100 years' duration.

The landscape in Czechoslovakia has changed through the influence of social, material and cultural developments past and present. This can be seen in attempts of Štěpánek z Netolic and Jakub Krčín to cultivate the landscape with advantage in the first half of the sixteenth century.

50

Through their work, an extensive system of canals and ponds came into existence in South Bohemia, giving this region a specific character which still exists because the area is protected by the Office for the State Protection of Nature.

The discovery of numerous mineral sources in Bohemia, Moravia and Slovakia and the knowledge of their curative effects led to the development in the first half of the nineteenth century of well-known spas, such as Františkovy Lázně, Mariánské Lázně, Karlovy Vary, Piešťany, etc. Their cultural and natural character has left an indelible imprint on the broader human environment.

## State protection of nature

The Czechoslovak Socialist Republic is characterized by a relatively high density of population in towns, settlements and municipalities. In spite of being an industrialized country, it has unspoilt regions which are ideal for relaxation and recreation. One-third of the territory is covered by forests, parks and gardens. However, the total proportion of open land, which amounts to more than 3,000 $m^2$ per inhabitant, works rather to the benefit of those who live in hill country; in industrial centres and towns there is only 40–300 $m^2$ per inhabitant. Czechoslovakia has the same problems in connection with the protection of the natural environment and natural resources as the other industrially developed European countries. In addition to a number of state organs concerned with the exploitation and protection of individual natural resources and the landscape as a whole, the Office for the State Protection of Nature has a specific role. It co-operates with a number of specialized and scientific institutions which participate in the protection of nature, not only in Czechoslovakia but also abroad, within the framework of the CMEA and Unesco. Its main task is to watch over the generative aspect of nature; thus the principal concern of the protection of nature office is not simply to save the protected territories from economic exploitation, but also to protect the natural environment in the process of its evolution.

## Protected territories

The principal activity of the Office for the State Protection of Nature consists in the creation of a network of protected territories. Their selection, categorization and exploitation is laid down on a strictly scientific basis. According to the Acts on the State Protection of Nature, there are several categories of specially protected territories. Large territories are declared national parks and protected landscape territories, smaller territories are declared state nature preserves, protected archaeological sites, protected parks, protected study areas and protected natural formations. Among the best known and most frequently visited protected territories are the Krkonoše National Park and the Tatra Mountains National Park. The Tatra Mountains National Park, founded in 1948, protects the unique region of the Czechoslovak Western Carpathian Mountains, which is comparable in character to the Alps.

The second biggest national park, the Krkonoše National Park, was founded in 1963. It contains the highest Czech mountains and has some very interesting scenery. Among other national parks, we should mention the Low Tatra Mountains and the Pieniny Mountains. The object in protecting these territories is to preserve their general landscape character, their physical features and important plant and animal species. Their importance lies in their recreational, cultural and educational opportunities.

## Education in the protection of nature

The Office for the State Protection of Nature also disseminates ideas and information on the comprehensive protection of the environment. To preserve the cultural and natural heritage there is no more effective and economical method than prevention. The cultural education of individuals, in this sense, is regarded as one of the most important aspects of the protection of nature.

The administrative authorities of large protected territories, apart from their conservation work, also have a cultural and educational function, which is demonstrated in their projects for children and youth. Examples are the summer camps, organized mostly in the national parks, the conservationist work teams and the international work camps. For a wider public, guided walks with an explanation provided by a fields guide or a guide-book have proved to be of great value. Useful educational work is performed by the field guides, who provide information and act as guides and supervisors.

Some social organizations also contribute to cultural education. For example, the Czech Union of the Protectors of Nature and the Slovak Union of the Protectors of Nature are voluntary organizations founded in 1979 which help develop citizens' activities for the protection of nature. The Socialist Union of Youth organizes movements such as the 'Brontosaurus'. Its goal is to involve young people in practical projects for the protection of nature, and to give the widest possible public a positive attitude to nature and the environment.

# Artists

The Art Unions play an important part in Czechoslovak cultural life. The Union of Czechoslovak Writers, the Union of Czechoslovak Dramatic Artists, the Union of Czechoslovak Composers, the Union of Czechoslovak Artists and the Union of Czechoslovak Architects are ideological and creative organizations, in which artists are associated on the basis of their common ideological and artistic programmes.

Through the organization of different meetings for artists, such as seminars, conferences, etc., continual contact between art workers is maintained for the solution of fundamental creative problems. There are also friendly discussions, authors' evenings, concerts, thematic exhibitions, shows, etc., which bring the artists into contact with the widest public. The Art Unions keep in constant touch with foreign colleagues, with whom there is a continual exchange of visits and information. They are also regularly represented at different international events and competitions.

It should be mentioned that the membership of Art Unions consists not only of the artists themselves, but also of scientific workers, theoreticians and publicists. The structure of Art Unions corresponds to that of the individual branches in the various fields. For example, the Union of Czechoslovak Composers brings together 188 composers of serious music, 126 composers of popular music, 383 concert artists, and 164 musicologists. Similarly, the Union of Czechoslovak Artists associates painters, sculptors, graphic designers, workers in the arts and crafts, and theoreticians; and the Union of Czechoslovak Dramatic Artists brings together actors, stage directors, dramatists, theatre theoreticians and film, radio and television artists. In the Union of Czechoslovak Writers, besides the authors of fiction, there are representatives from other contemporary literary branches, literary theoreticians and critics.

The cultural press is the concern of the Art Unions, along with scientific and professional institutions and social organizations. Specialized journals, popular magazines and the daily press give coverage to literature, the fine arts, music, the theatre and to dramatic productions in general. Out of 1,040 periodicals published in Czechoslovakia 132 are devoted to cultural and artistic questions.

## Education of the Young Generation of Artistic and Cultural Workers

### UNIVERSITIES AND COLLEGES

In Czechoslovakia, a system of secondary schools and institutions of higher learning, where young artists are prepared for creative activity in all the art disciplines has been developing for almost 200 years (see Table 5). These schools cover not only the needs of Czech and Slovak students, but also accept a number of foreign students. The oldest institution of this type is the Academy of Fine Arts in Prague, founded in 1800. At this school, painting, sculpture, graphic art, architecture and art restoration are taught. Another school with a rich tradition is the School of Arts and Crafts in Prague which originated in 1885. This school has regularly displayed Czechoslovak applied art on the international scene (for example Paris 1925, Stockholm 1931, Brussels 1958, etc.). The range of subjects studied at this school includes stage design, exhibition design, interior design, the working and human environment, applied painting, applied sculpture, design of machines and instruments, ceramics, china, utility glass, jewellery, textile design, dress design, book design and type design, publicity and posters, film and television graphic art, illustration and applied graphic art.

In the Slovak Socialist Republic there is the School of Fine Arts in Bratislava, founded in 1949, which fulfils the function of both the Prague schools and prepares students in similar art disciplines.

The institution of higher learning for music and dramatic art is the Academy of Music and Dramatic Art in Prague, founded in 1945, with the following faculties and study branches: Theatre Faculty (acting, stage direction and drama, theatre organization and management, stage designing and puppetry); Faculty of Music (composition, conducting, opera directing, singing, string instruments, wind instruments, keyboard instruments, choreography); Film and Television Faculty (film and television drama and screen-writing, film and television directing, film and television camera-work, film and television production, art photography). There are institutions of higher learning with a similar study programme in Brno—the Janáček Academy of Music and Dramatic Art (founded in 1947) and in Bratislava—the School of Music and Dramatic Art (founded in 1959).

The students at these schools have at their disposal special stages and concert halls where they present the results of their study to the

TABLE 5. Development of the number of students at art-oriented institutions of higher learning in the Czechoslovak Socialist Republic, 1965–80

| School year | Total number of students | Academy of Music and Dramatic Art in Prague | Janáček Academy of Music and Dramatic Art in Brno | School of Music and Dramatic Art in Bratislava | Academy of Fine Arts in Prague | School of Fine Arts in Bratislava | School of Arts and Crafts in Prague | Total number of foreign students |
|---|---|---|---|---|---|---|---|---|
| 1960 | 1 225 | 445 | 128 | 173 | 117 | 110 | 252 | 90 |
| 1965 | 1 744 | 685 | 226 | 209 | 131 | 158 | 335 | 113 |
| 1970 | 1 863 | 753 | 231 | 228 | 183 | 213 | 255 | 121 |
| 1975 | 2 029 | 850 | 205 | 282 | 219 | 194 | 279 | 115 |
| 1980 | 2 191 | 867 | 230 | 361 | 226 | 186 | 321 | 98 |

public. They participate in competitions and festivals abroad, where their performances are as a rule very much appreciated.

The graduates of the art-oriented institutions of higher learning work in the extensive network of Czechoslovak art and cultural institutions—in philharmonic orchestras, theatres, film and television studios. For artists there are many opportunities for participating in the system of competitions for which entries are invited by state and social organizations, in the network of exhibition halls and art galleries throughout the country, and the art galleries of the Dílo Art Fund. When designing new housing and public buildings, provision is always made to decorate them with works of art. Industrial design is also a large field of activity for artists.

Specialists with university qualifications in the theory and practice of culture and art are given further training at the faculties of arts of individual universities, namely the Charles University in Prague, the Palacký University in Olomouc, the J. E. Purkyně University in Brno, the Komenský University in Bratislava and the P. J. Šafařík University in Košice.

At the faculties of arts, the cultural workers of the future study for the most part in the following departments: history of art, aesthetics, music, drama and film science, theory of culture, adult education, sociology, ethnography, folklore, librarianship and scientific information. The graduates in these disciplines make their impact in scientific and research activity, literary journalism and criticism, as workers and organizers of cultural life in houses of culture and clubs, in libraries, etc.

### SECONDARY SCHOOLS

The system of secondary art schools in Czechoslovakia also has a rich and fruitful tradition. The oldest school of this type is the Prague Conservatoire, founded in 1811. There are ten conservatories where the following disciplines can be studied: keyboard, string, wind, percussion and folk instruments, solo singing, composition, conducting, acting and dancing.

At the secondary vocational schools with an art orientation, specialists are educated in the following branches of applied art: industrial design, advertising, metal work, ceramics, glass, textiles, stone and imitation jewellery, clothing and footwear design, arts and crafts, packaging, graphic design, window dressing, photography, conservation and restoration. (See Table 6 for a breakdown of the numbers involved.)

An original aspect of some of these schools is that they have been founded in places that are closely connected with their field of study, due to the presence of the necessary raw material (for example, the School of Glass Industry in Nový Bor, the School of Ceramics in Karlovy Vary, the School of the Stone Cutting Industry in Hořice), or which are the traditional home of a certain industry (imitation jewellery in Jablonec nad Nisou, glass in Železný Brod, metal and stone-working in Turnov, etc.).

Cultural workers with secondary-school qualifications are educated

56

Artists

**TABLE 6.**  Students at secondary schools
with an art orientation, 1975–80

|  | School year | |
|---|---|---|
| Branch | 1975 | 1980 |
| Woodwork and production of musical instruments | 2 585 | 2 626 |
| Printing trade, paper-making, films and photography | 685 | 691 |
| Literary journalism, librarianship and scientific information | 1 555 | 1 880 |
| Art, applied art and art handicrafts | 6 186 | 6 727 |

**TABLE 7.**  Students at secondary librarian schools
and conservatories, 1960–80

|  | School year | | | | |
|---|---|---|---|---|---|
|  | 1960 | 1965 | 1970 | 1975 | 1980 |
| Secondary librarian schools | 938 | 1 501 | 1 748 | 1 977 | 2 200 |
| Conservatories | 1 846 | 2 975 | 2 869 | 3 296 | 3 441 |

mostly at grammar schools and at secondary librarian schools (see Table 7) where extension courses are organized for such disciplines as scientific and technological documentation, and cultural and educational work. School-leavers work as organizers and methodological workers in state, trade union and other cultural institutions. In the field of secondary-school education for cultural workers, post-secondary courses are of great importance in improving and extending qualifications in special subjects and enlarging upon the knowledge gained during secondary-school studies. This type of study is the responsibility of the Institute for Cultural and Educational Activity attached to the Ministry of Culture of the Czech Socialist Republic in Prague and of the Institute for Adult Education attached to the Ministry of Culture of the Slovak Socialist Republic in Bratislava. The education of voluntary cultural workers is organized by cultural centres that exist in all regions and districts of the Czechoslovak Socialist Republic. Further education of managers in the field of culture is organized by the Institute for the Education of Workers in Culture and Art in Prague and by the Institute for the Education of Workers in Culture in Bratislava.

## ARTS AND CRAFTS

The socialist state pays systematic attention to the preservation of traditional arts and crafts, which are of great importance both for the upkeep and restoration of historic buildings and their interiors, and for beautifying the human environment. For these demanding professions, young people can serve the following apprenticeships: artsmith, locksmith girdle-maker, cabinet-maker, upholsterer, decorator, woodworker, worker with natural materials, ceramicist, glassworker, gilder, glazier, tapestry-weaver, hand-weaver, hand-embroiderer, hand lace-worker, textile printer, art interior painter, stucco-worker, wig-maker, stage-costume tailor. Young people who have served their apprenticeship in these branches work in the Arts and Crafts Centre and in a number of co-operative organizations concerned with arts-and-crafts production.

This complete education system for the preparation of workers in individual branches of artistic and cultural activities at all levels—from skilled workers and cultural organizers to creative artists and scientific and research workers—is the result of historical development, and of systematic care by the state and the whole of society.

# Cultural life of the population

The national plan setting out the main tasks to be accomplished in the field of culture is discussed regularly and approved by the Czech and Slovak Governments; the Czech National Council, the Slovak National Council and the Federal Assembly also follow the results of these discussions. The Revolutionary Trade Union Movement, the Socialist Union of Youth, both national Unions of Women as well as other popular and specialized organizations include cultural and educational activities in their programmes.

Cultural needs and interests occupy an important position in the Czechoslovak way of life. To satisfy these needs, extensive and varied cultural and educational facilities exist in practically every municipality, and influence the lifestyle in the following particular ways: they facilitate social activities and contacts, enrich the spiritual life of citizens, and encourage the appropriate use of leisure and the development of hobbies. They encourage a deeper perception of cultural and artistic values, influence the formation of ideological attitudes and value orientation, and inspire positive transformations in life-style, housing, etc.

The national committees are mainly responsible for the development of cultural and educational activities in their province, and supervise it according to a plan which includes the activities of the cultural facilities of the relevant committee and also those of non-governmental organizations. At district and regional level, there are cultural centres whose particular task is to assist in controlling and organizing the activity of local cultural facilities. At national level, in the Czech Socialist Republic and the Slovak Socialist Republic, the central methodological places of work are the specialized institutes of both national Ministries of Culture.

Cultural and educational activity comprises the two basic components of education and leisure.

## Adult education and youth education

The beginnings of adult education in Czechoslovakia go back to the
last century, when university extra-mural classes were first organized
by the professors of the Charles University in 1899. Various associations
also organized educational activities, such as the Workers' Academy, etc.
At national level, this activity was organized from 1906 by the Union for
Adult Education. Adult education was thus based in the first place on the
initiative of individual leisure and professional associations and corporations.

This has only achieved a status of national importance and interest
in the stage of the socialist development of the Czechoslovak state when,
in the spirit of a uniform system of education, it was formed into a complete
network consisting of three basic subsystems:
1. *School system* within the framework of which citizens may receive
   higher education in the form of extra-mural, part-time studies at
   secondary schools and at the institutions of higher learning (see Tables 8,
   9 and 10).
2. Education of employees in *organizations* (i.e. at the establishments
   where they work) which satisfies practical needs and contributes to raising
   the professional qualifications of the working population in all branches
   of the national economy.

TABLE 8.  Studies at secondary schools
for the working population, 1975–81

| School year | Total number of students | Evening courses | Divided into cycles | Extra-mural courses |
|---|---|---|---|---|
| 1975 | 4 024 | 4 024 | — | — |
| 1980 | 34 754 | 25 741 | 8 890 | 123 |
| 1981 | 31 309 | 21 943 | 7 721 | 1 645 |

TABLE 9.  Extra-mural courses at institutions
of higher learning, 1960–80

| School year | Total number of students | Proportion of working students |
|---|---|---|
| 1960 | 84 040 | 26 740 |
| 1965 | 144 990 | 49 967 |
| 1970 | 131 099 | 25 465 |
| 1975 | 154 645 | 32 018 |
| 1980 | 196 642 | 45 138 |

TABLE 10.　　　Studies for the working population
at secondary vocational schools
and at vocational schools, 1970–80

| School year | Total number of students |
|---|---|
| 1970 | 67 507 |
| 1975 | 94 470 |
| 1980 | 88 168 |

3. Out-of-school education, implemented in the *network of cultural and educational facilities* of the national committees, which are state institutions, and also in the facilities of social organizations, particularly the Trade Union Movement. This educational subsystem includes an extensive range of possibilities. The system of out-of-school education satisfies the different cultural and educational interests of citizens, improves their general as well as their professional education, and helps them to adapt to changing living and working conditions (see Tables 11 and 12). An important feature of out-of-school education, in comparison with the school system, is thematic and subject freedom, close connection with life, and the way in which it is adapted to the needs of society and to local and individual needs. Out-of-school education is accessible to every citizen during his or her lifetime, and thus our society puts

TABLE 11.　　　Individual educational activities of state
and non-state organizations
(Branches: Marxist-Leninist philosophy, science
and technology, civics, working education
and improving general education, aesthetic education,
physical training, language education)

| Year | Number of actions | Number of participants |
|---|---|---|
| 1975 | 150 435 | 14 954 315 |
| 1980 | 553 963 | 25 117 691 |
| 1983 | 589 647 | 27 209 043 |

TABLE 12.　　　Cyclic educational activities of state
and non-state organizations (same branches as Table 11)

| Year | Number of lecture cycles | Number of lectures | Number of leavers |
|---|---|---|---|
| 1975 | 16 058 | 79 887 | 761 638 |
| 1980 | — | 74 496 | 2 537 628 |
| 1983 | — | 109 737 | 3 425 746 |

into practice the postulate of Comenius, expressed in his work *Pampaedia*: 'No age is too old for learning, for it must be said: every age is appropriate for learning and the limits for life are the only limits for learning.' The main stimuli for participation in out-of-school education are the desire for self-education and development of the personality, and the need to obtain the most recent knowledge on a certain subject. The highest organs in charge of out-of-school education are the National Commissions for Adult Education, situated within the framework of the Czech Ministry of culture and the Slovak Ministry of Culture. The main responsibility, control and co-ordinative function in out-of-school education lie with the National Ministries of Culture and the national committees. The Regional National Committees and the District National Committees constitute, in co-operation with social and co-operative organizations, the councils for out-of-school education.

In this field, the societies for the popularization of science, particularly the Socialist Academy and the Czechoslovak Scientific and Technological Society—voluntary associations of scientific and specialized workers from different branches, who work as lecturers—have an important role to play.

The cultural education of children and youth has a particularly important place. On a state-wide scale, the co-ordinated system, Youth and Culture, has been introduced, organized by the District Houses of Culture and schools, from apprentice schools to grammar schools. The essence of this system is to acquaint children and young people in general with cultural, artistic and historical values directly linked with the school curricula. During the school year, children and young people. even from the most remote places, attend dramatic performances, concerts, cinemas, participate in excursions to historic monuments, and so on. The learning process at school is enriched through the arts. The considerable expense involved in the implementation of the Youth and Culture system (reduced admission fees, excursions to theatres, etc., which are free of charge in all municipalities) are covered from the budgets of the national committees and also by the local trade union organizations where the school is located.

The art education of the youngest children is also ensured by the network of people's schools of art (see Table 13), for which pupils are selectep according to their talent in the last year of nursery school (i. e. at the age of 5.) There are at present 490 schools of this type and more than 210,000 pupils are educated in them in the fields of music, dancing, fine arts,

TABLE 13.　　　　　Students at the people's schools of art, 1971–84

|  | 1971 | 1975 | 1980 | 1984 |
|---|---|---|---|---|
| Schools | 438 | 465 | 490 | 496 |
| Pupils | 136 920 | 184 938 | 211 239 | 214 156 |

TABLE 14.                   Students according to individual branches, 1978–80

|                           | 1978    | 1980    |
|---------------------------|---------|---------|
| Dancing                   | 18 640  | 20 930  |
| Fine arts                 | 36 025  | 40 635  |
| Literary and dramatic art | 5 330   | 6 712   |
| Music                     | 139 580 | 142 962 |
| TOTAL                     | 199 574 | 211 239 |

literature and dramatic art (see Table 14). The cultural and educational facilities of the National Committees and Trade Unions also organize similar courses of art education for children not attending the people's schools of art. For all members of the youngest generation there are favourable conditions for training in the main fields of art.

## Hobbies

To develop creative activities for citizens in their leisure time, the state and the trade union cultural and educational authorities provide the necessary facilities. There are two basic fields—art, and science and technology, etc. (see Table 15). The socialist state fully supports cultural

TABLE 15.                   Hobbies of the population
                            of the Czechoslovak Socialist Republic, 1957–83

| Year | Number of ensembles and groups | Number of members |
|------|--------------------------------|-------------------|
| *Art hobbies* | | |
| 1957 | 11 428 | 207 563 |
| 1960 | 11 102 | 178 707 |
| 1965 | 20 544 | 331 715 |
| 1970 | 16 921 | 276 095 |
| 1975 | 26 264 | 463 224 |
| 1980 | 31 200 | 551 350 |
| 1981 | 32 764 | 563 742 |
| 1982 | 33 535 | 595 849 |
| 1983 | 34 668 | 616 262 |
| *'Non-art' hobbies* | | |
| 1957 | 5 916  | 85 323  |
| 1960 | 5 275  | 77 464  |
| 1965 | 14 270 | 135 254 |
| 1970 | 11 084 | 132 657 |
| 1975 | 25 473 | 331 378 |
| 1980 | 25 353 | 342 650 |
| 1981 | 30 685 | 407 545 |
| 1982 | 31 414 | 424 599 |
| 1983 | 33 111 | 474 563 |

TABLE 16.                    Participation of the population in art hobbies, 1975–83

| Branch or group | 1975 | | 1980 | | 1983 | |
|---|---|---|---|---|---|---|
| | Ensembles | Members | Ensembles | Members | Ensembles | Members |
| Theatre | 3 100 | 58 537 | 3 687 | 61 982 | 2 706 | 49 325 |
| Puppetry | 623 | 8 861 | 863 | 11 609 | 962 | 12 854 |
| Songs and dances | 1 738 | 37 228 | 1 796 | 40 128 | 2 087 | 48 251 |
| Choirs | 3 083 | 84 706 | 3 605 | 102 000 | 3 752 | 105 658 |
| Music | 3 118 | 32 931 | —[1] | — | — | — |
| Folk bands | 3 955 | 41 373 | —[1] | — | — | — |
| Recitations | 2 036 | 24 042 | —[1] | — | — | — |
| Mixed art groups | 615 | 9 474 | —[1] | — | — | — |
| Photography | 2 145 | 22 934 | 3 022 | 31 082 | 3 049 | 31 483 |
| Films | 415 | 3 464 | 498 | 5 981 | 547 | 6 658 |
| Fine arts | 1 534 | 20 135 | 2 369 | 37 549 | 2 660 | 40 439 |
| Folk-art production | 248 | 3 744 | 458 | 6 552 | 580 | 8 600 |
| Clubs of the friends of art | 343 | 45 400 | 635 | 63 591 | 878 | 72 842 |
| Ballroom dancing | 529 | 13 259 | 879 | 18 307 | 1 065 | 21 387 |
| Other branches | 2 782 | 57 136 | 5 962 | 94 491 | 310 | 4 451 |
| TOTAL | 26 264 | 463 224 | 31 200 | 551 350 | 34 668 | 616 262 |
| Symphonic music | —[1] | — | 229 | 4 118[1] | 310 | 4 451 |
| Dance music | —[1] | — | 5 052 | 35 015 | 5 274 | 36 638 |
| Wind music | —[1] | — | 1 948 | 36 063 | 1 863 | 37 071 |
| Folk songs and dances | —[1] | — | 1 796 | 40 128 | 2 087 | 48 251 |

1. Name of statistical indices changed.

creative activity, because it is one of the fundamental necessities for the development of the individual and of society as a whole.

The first amateur dramatic ensembles appeared two centuries ago and folk bands have a still longer tradition—they existed in rural areas in the Baroque period and their music even influenced, to a certain extent, the work of some important composers. At that time, too, Bohemia became known as the conservatory of Europe.

In the present social conditions, these traditions of amateur performances of plays and music continue to develop and to occupy a leading position in the list of hobbies of an artistic character. They can be subdivided as follows: theatre, puppetry, singing, symphonic music, dance music, wind music, folk songs and dances, recitation, photography, films, fine arts, folk-art production, art and ballroom dancing (see Table 16).

Citizens are associated in their spare time with more than 34,000 ensembles and groups with more than 600,000 members (see Tables 15 and 16). There are also a large number of individual amateur authors and artists who, of course, cannot be statistically registered.

The cultural centres in the regions and districts send their methodological workers to these ensembles and offer them positive assistance in their activities. Material equipment (for example, musical instruments, costumes, studios, etc.) is also provided from the funds of the National Committees and social organizations. Professional artists—actors, painters and sculptors, writers—also give the amateur ensembles advice and help. The activity of amateur ensembles is stimulated by the system of regional and national competitions and performances and the best ensembles also represent Czechoslovakia abroad. As regards this aspect, considerable changes can be seen in comparison with the pre-socialist period, when a great number of different amateur ensembles were set up as companies, having to depend entirely upon the subscriptions of their members and profits from public performances.

In the present stage of scientific and technological development, hobbies of a 'non-art' nature are becoming more important and more widespread. Currently, 470,000 participants in this type of activity are organized in more than 33,000 groups (see Table 17). Hobby teams specializing in local geography, natural sciences, astronomy, technology, agriculture, visual propaganda and PA systems have been created.

From some of these activities, ideas emerge which are useful not only for the development of an individual, but also of society. Scientific and technological leisure-time activities are assessed by the 'improvers' movement' which considers ideas in all sectors of the national economy. Participants in these hobbies present the results of their work at regional and national exhibitions and competitions for technological creative activity.

TABLE 17.    Participation of the population in 'non-art' hobbies, 1975–83

| Branch or group | 1975 | | 1980 | | 1983 | |
|---|---|---|---|---|---|---|
| | Ensembles | Members | Ensembles | Members | Ensembles | Members |
| Local geography | 740 | 18 161 | 992 | 18 610 | 1 386 | 27 181 |
| Natural sciences | 1 187 | 23 923 | 2 410 | 34 444 | 3 169 | 58 531 |
| Astronomy | 309 | 4 958 | 552 | 9 343 | 851 | 12 941 |
| Technology | 1 758 | 30 130 | 2 654 | 39 160 | 4 222 | 68 381 |
| Agriculture | 470 | 11 135 | 512 | 10 435 | 498 | 9 645 |
| Visual propaganda | 4 237 | 23 080 | 4 315 | 25 367 | 5 141 | 29 493 |
| PA systems and radio | 4 317 | 24 062 | 4 541 | 26 829 | 5 095 | 26 951 |
| Bodies for civic affairs | 6 273 | 46 725 | — | — | — | — |
| Other groups | 6 182 | 149 204 | 9 378 | 169 462 | 12 749 | 254 189 |
| TOTAL | 25 473 | 331 378 | 25 354 | 342 650 | 33 111 | 474 563 |

## Cultural life of national minorities

The Czechoslovak Socialist Republic is a state consisting of two equal nations, the Czechs and the Slovaks. Several other ethnic groups live in the country and their legal status is laid down in the Constitution. Equal rights for all citizens, regardless of ethnic group and race, are guaranteed by Article 20 of the Constitution of 1960 as well as by the Constitutional Act (No. 144/1968) concerning the Status of Ethnic Groups int he Czechoslovak Socialist Republic, promulgated 'in the endeavour to extend and further strengthen the fraternal coexistence and solidarity of nations and ethnic groups and secure the participation of citizens of other national origins in the exercise of state power and to provide them with effective guarantees of their continued progress'.

This Act concerns explicitly the Hungarian, Polish, German and Ukrainian national minorities who are also guaranteed appropriate representation in the elected bodies. The above-mentioned ethnic groups are specifically guaranteed,

to the extent appropriate in the interests of their ethnic development and under conditions specified by law, the right to education in their own language, the right to all-round cultural development, the right to use their language in official communications in areas inhabited by the respective ethnic groups, the right to associate in ethnic cultural and social organizations, the right to their own press and to information in their own language [Article 3 of the above-mentioned Act].

On the territory of the Czechoslovak Socialist Republic, there are about 582,000 citizens of Hungarian national origin, 69,000 of Polish origin, 60,000 of German origin and 47,000 of Ukrainian origin. In the spirit of this Act, the following associations were founded: the Cultural Association of the Hungarian Working Population in the Czechoslovak Socialist Republic, the Polish Cultural and Educational Union, the Cultural Association of the Citizens of German Origin in the Czechoslovak Socialist Republic, and the Cultural Union of the Ukrainian Working Population in the Czechoslovak Socialist Republic. To choose freely a certain nation or ethnic group is the right of every Czechoslovak citizen; the state and its organs must respect this decision. Citizens choose for themselves the schools to which they wish to send their children, the mother tongue the child will use, and in which cultural climate the child should be educated. The state is obliged to create the conditions necessary for this. Being a member of a particular ethnic group does not work to the detriment of any citizen in his or her participation in political, economic and cultural life.

Publishing plays an important role in the development of the life of national minorities. Each of the above-mentioned unions and associations has the possibility of publishing literature for its members in its own language. This is mostly the original literature of the minority concerned; these publishing houses produce only re-editions of the literature of neighbouring countries on a small scale. Cultural centres have been established on the basis of inter-government agreements, where every citizen has the opportunity to purchase the desired literature. At the same time, all public libraries are obliged to hold an adequate stock of the literature of individual national minorities. Periodicals are also published in the four languages of these nationalities.

An important event for the national minorities are the all-union competitions, shows and festivals of amateur art activity which are a periodic demonstration of systematic care for the cultural life of individual ethnic groups in the Czechoslovak Socialist Republic. In the field of professional art, the theatre is of the greatest importance for the ethnic groups. The Polish, Ukrainian and Hungarian national minorities have their professional theatres (the Hungarian national minority has two theatres). German dramatic art is ensured by guest performances of ensembles from the German Democratic Republic. Of great importance also are the professional folklore ensembles.

In districts where a great number of citizens of national minorities live, the films of neighbouring nations are frequently projected in the original version, with Czech and Slovak subtitles. The mass media too reserve an appropriate share of their broadcasting time to carry news for national minorities in their mother tongue.

## Cultural and educational facilities

In Czechoslovakia, there are 6,500 cultural and educational facilities of the National Committees, 700 cultural facilities of the Revolutionary Trade Union Movement, 170 clubs of agricultural co-operatives, and almost 2,000 clubs of the Socialist Union of Youth, with a total number of visitors in 1983 of 112 million, which represents 3 visits per citizen per year (see Table 18). Tables 19–22 illustrate the use made of particular facilities, such as museums, art galleries and courses of study.

TABLE 18. Educational, cultural and social activity of cultural and educational facilities, 1966–83

| Year | Educational activity | | Cultural and social activity | |
|---|---|---|---|---|
| | Events | Visitors (1,000s) | Events | Visitors (1,000s) |
| 1966 | 128 850 | 5 969 | 235 934 | 39 827 |
| 1970 | 87 357 | 4 837 | 336 887 | 42 628 |
| 1975 | 250 435 | 14 954 | 395 387 | 81 802 |
| 1980 | 553 963 | 25 118 | 521 716 | 72 929 |
| 1981 | 589 647 | 26 887 | 570 053 | 79 547 |
| 1982 | 594 643 | 26 257 | 589 817 | — |
| 1983 | 662 681 | 27 209 | 603 185 | 85 647 |

# Cultural life of the population

TABLE 19.  Educational activity of cultural
and educational facilities (courses), 1957–80

| Year | Courses | Graduates |
|------|---------|-----------|
| 1957 | 7 246 | 185 292 |
| 1960 | 13 987 | 363 938 |
| 1965 | 23 843 | 462 662 |
| 1970 | 28 097 | 506 319 |
| 1975 | 39 330 | 681 366 |
| 1980 | 48 981 | 787 044 |

TABLE 20.  Index of the number of visitors to cultural
and educational facilities, 1960–83 (expressed as percentages)

| Year | Educational activity | | Cultural and social activity: visitors | Hobbies | | Educational activity: graduates |
|------|--------|----------|-----------|-----|---------|----------|
|      | Events | Visitors |           | Art | Non-art |          |
| 1960 | — | — | — | 100 | 100 | 100 (index) |
| 1966 | 100 | 100 | 100 | — | — | — |
| 1970 | 67.8 | 81.0 | 107.0 | 154.5 | 171.3 | 139.1 |
| 1975 | 194.4 | 250.5 | 205.4 | 259.2 | 427.8 | 187.2 |
| 1980 | 429.9 | 420.8 | 183.1 | 308.5 | 442.3 | 216.3 |
| 1981 | 457.6 | 450.4 | 199.7 | 315.5 | 526.1 | — |
| 1982 | 461.5 | 439.9 | — | 287.1 | 497.6 | — |
| 1983 | 467.7 | 455.8 | 215.4 | 344.8 | 612.6 | — |

TABLE 21.  Museums and the number of visitors, 1955–83

| Year | Museums including branch museums | Visitors (1,000s) | Index of number of visitors |
|------|----------------------------------|-------------------|------------------------------|
| 1955 | 421 | 3 725 | 100.0 (index) |
| 1960 | 378 | 6 247 | 167.6 |
| 1965 | 371 | 8 624 | 232.4 |
| 1970 | 401 | 8 333 | 225.1 |
| 1975 | 464 | 13 449 | 364.9 |
| 1980 | 505 | 16 384 | 442.7 |
| 1981 | 490 | 15 257 | 409.6 |
| 1982 | 503 | 13 833 | 378.8 |
| 1983 | 493 | 13 762 | 369.4 |

TABLE 22.  Art galleries, their collections, exhibition activity
and the number of visitors, 1955–83

| Year | Galleries | Exhibits | Exhibitions | Visitors (1,000s) | Index of number of visitors (%) | Exhibitions abroad |
|------|-----------|----------|-------------|-------------------|----------------------------------|---------------------|
| 1955 | 16 | 217 963 | 514 | 1 473.0 | 100.0 | — |
| 1960 | 19 | 487 676 | 1 016 | 2 758.0 | 187.3 | — |
| 1965 | 32 | 825 305 | 2 094 | 3 011.0 | 204.4 | — |
| 1970 | 39 | 727 080 | 1 705 | 2 405.0 | 163.3 | — |
| 1975 | 38 | 705 900 | 2 427 | 3 335.8 | 226.5 | 50 |
| 1980 | 40 | 860 615 | 2 545 | 5 347.0 | 371.5 | 44 |
| 1981 | 41 | 869 867 | 2 255 | 4 863.3 | 330.1 | 29 |
| 1982 | 42 | — | 2 156 | 4 908.0 | 333.2 | 42 |
| 1983 | 42 | — | 2 310 | 5 220.0 | 354.4 | 63 |

TABLE 23.  Network and book collections of people's libraries, 1950–83

| Year | Libraries | Branch libraries | Books (1,000s) |
|------|-----------|------------------|----------------|
| 1950 | 14 474 | 657 | 11 095 |
| 1955 | 14 405 | 519 | 15 405 |
| 1960 | 13 836 | 718 | 20 802 |
| 1965 | 12 667 | 1 610 | 27 850 |
| 1970 | 11 245 | 2 308 | 32 856 |
| 1975 | 11 116 | 1 940 | 41 618 |
| 1980 | 10 157 | 2 265 | 50 590 |
| 1981 | 9 900 | 2 392 | 47 965 |
| 1982 | 9 776 | 2 429 | 51 500 |
| 1983 | 9 760 | 2 335 | 52 821 |

TABLE 24.  Index of the development of book collections, readers
and loans in public libraries, 1950–83
(expressed as percentages)

| Year | Book collections | Readers[1] | Loans |
|------|------------------|------------|-------|
| 1950 | 100.0 | 100.0 | 100.0 |
| 1955 | 138.8 | 142.2 | 148.3 |
| 1960 | 187.5 | 148.9 | 108.6 |
| 1965 | 251.0 | 159.8 | 219.1 |
| 1970 | 296.1 | 154.9 | 245.8 |
| 1975 | 375.1 | 196.2 | 315.9 |
| 1980 | 459.2 | 231.6 | 405.6 |
| 1981 | 432.3 | 232.0 | 404.9 |
| 1983 | 476.1 | 243.8 | 422.3 |

1. According to the number of readers' cards.

In the Czechoslovak Socialist Republic, regional, district and local people's libraries have been established in almost all municipalities (see Table 23). Because it is a uniform network, every citizen has the facility of borrowing any publication through the inter-library and international loan service (see Tables 24 and 25 for levels of reader activity). In addition to the network of public libraries, Czechoslovakia has an extensive network of libraries of the Revolutionary Trade Union Movement (about 8,500 libraries), more than 9,000 school libraries, 19 state scientific libraries (see Table 26), 1,696 university, technological and other libraries.

TABLE 25.  Participation of the population in the activity of people's libraries, 1955–83

| Year | Inhabitants per library | Books per 1,000 inhabitants | Readers[1] | Loans | |
|------|------|------|------|------|------|
| | | | | Total | Per reader[1] |
| 1955 | 881.9 | 117.0 | 12.3 | 28 141 | 19.4 |
| 1960 | 941.2 | 151.9 | 12.3 | 38 071 | 22.5 |
| 1965 | 994.2 | 196.2 | 12.8 | 40 181 | 25.1 |
| 1970 | 1 060.0 | 228.7 | 12.2 | 51 815 | 29.5 |
| 1975 | 1 137.9 | 280.1 | 15.0 | 67 139 | 29.9 |
| 1980 | 1 230.3 | 331.0 | 17.2 | 85 491 | 32.6 |
| 1983 | 1 581.7 | 345.6 | 18.1 | 89 015 | 32.2 |

1. According to the number of readers' cards.

TABLE 26.  Numbers and use of state scientific libraries, 1960–83

| Year | Libraries | Volumes (1,000s) | Readers |
|------|------|------|------|
| 1960 | 14 | 8 492 | 100 212 |
| 1965 | 13 | 12 000 | 150 321 |
| 1970 | 14 | 14 832 | 159 000 |
| 1975 | 14 | 18 409 | 186 015 |
| 1980 | 15 | 26 608 | 261 967 |
| 1981 | 19 | 29 132 | 349 381 |
| 1982 | 19 | 30 541 | 337 035 |
| 1983 | 22 | 32 574 | 361 171 |

# The mass media

Films, Radio and Television in Czechoslovakia are independent, state-wide organizations, the control of which falls within the competence of the Federal Government and its organs.

Each of these institutions has its own headquarters and its central director. They have independent national studios, but they also come together for common productions. Often, Czech actors and film-makers participate in Slovak film and television production and vice versa. Radio and television studios broadcast on Czech and Slovak channels and also on the state-wide programme covering both nations.

## Cinema

The high level of Czechoslovak cinema, television and radio production can be seen at different competitions and festivals, in the export of films and in the mutual exchange of programmes. The film industry has a

TABLE 27.    Cinema of the National Committees, film performances and number of visitors, 1960–83

| Year | Total number of cinemas | Cinemas with wide screens | Cinemas with 70 mm screens | Performances | Visitors (1,000s) | Index of number of visitors |
|------|------|------|------|------|------|------|
| 1960 | 3 566 | 322 | — | 1 090 000 | 176 465 | 100.0 |
| 1965 | 3 711 | 641 | — | 1 045 000 | 128 404 | 72.8 |
| 1970 | 3 496 | 898 | 53 | 930 000 | 114 751 | 65.0 |
| 1975 | 3 404 | 1 087 | 76 | 876 000 | 85 861 | 48.3 |
| 1980 | 3 084 | 1 168 | 87 | 812 000 | 82 310 | 46.6 |
| 1981 | 2 981 | 1 193 | 86 | 798 000 | 80 993 | 45.8 |
| 1982 | 2 891 | 1 219 | 86 | 778 000 | 78 575 | 44.5 |
| 1983 | 2 866 | 1 204 | 87 | 766 000 | 76 487 | 43.3 |

relatively well-equipped production location in the well-known Barrandov film studios. In the 1930s, they began making films with directors such as G. Machatý, films which shunned commercial aims. Later Czechoslovak films were presented successfully for the first time at world festivals. *The Guild of Kutná Hora Virgins* by Otakar Vávra won the Luce Golden Cup in 1938 in Venice, and *The Siren* by Karel Stekly won the Grand Prix, the Golden Lion, also in Venice in 1947. This film symbolically opened the new road that Czechoslovak cinema has taken since nationalization in 1945. At present some 60 full-length films and more than 200 animated cartoons are produced in Czechoslovakia every year. Total film production covers about 1,500 titles annually, produced for the distribution network of the traditional cinema as well as for television (see Table 28). Most titles are also exported, to about thirty countries in all (see Table 29). For many years now Czechoslovak films have been among the leading works of world production, winning prizes at different international festivals (Cannes, Trieste, Moscow, Karlovy Vary, Chicago, San Sebastian, Tehran,

TABLE 28. Films produced, 1957–83

| Year | Total films produced | Full-length films | Medium-length and short films | News films |
|------|------|------|------|------|
| 1957 | 709 | 27 | 488 | 199 |
| 1960 | 917 | 36 | 646 | 235 |
| 1965 | 912 | 45 | 659 | 208 |
| 1970 | 1 257 | 54 | 1 020 | 183 |
| 1975 | 1 643 | 62 | 1 420 | 161 |
| 1980 | 1 788 | 73 | 1 543 | 172 |
| 1981 | 1 654 | 62 | 1 421 | 171 |
| 1982 | 1 660 | 60 | 1 427 | 173 |
| 1983 | 1 501 | 66 | 1 269 | 166 |

TABLE 29. Development of film imports and exports, 1945–82

| Year | Imported films | | Exported films | |
|------|------|------|------|------|
| | Full-length | Short | Full-length | Short |
| 1945 | 42 | — | — | — |
| 1950 | 45 | 85 | 98 | 113 |
| 1955 | 97 | 150 | 150 | 366 |
| 1960 | 173 | 99 | 176 | 322 |
| 1965 | 140 | 150 | 408 | 555 |
| 1970 | 184 | 135 | 245 | 574 |
| 1975 | 233 | 176 | 241 | 692 |
| 1980 | 172 | 91 | 446 | 826 |
| 1981 | 186 | 112 | 446 | 764 |
| 1982 | 155 | 57 | 405 | 846 |

Carthage, etc.). The relatively strong upward trend in the quality of Czechoslovak cinema in post-war years and its international successes are connected with the names of its most successful film directors, such as O. Vávra, K. Steklý, M. Frič, J. Sequens, J. Spitzer, J. Jakubisko, Z. Podskalský, J. Roháč, K. Kachyňa, F. Vláčil, A. Kachlík, J. Menzel and others.

In Czechoslovakia, a number of national and international film festivals take place (for example Ekofilm, Tourfilm, Techfilm, films for children and youth, etc.) prominent among which is the International Film Festival in Karlovy Vary. Within its framework, directors from all continents regularly make their debut. Another remarkable event is the Film Festival of the Working People which has taken place regularly for thirty-five years. It has the character of a popular summer festival, in open-air cinemas with a capacity of ten thousand spectators who have the chance to meet delegations of film directors and actors.

Film experts and fans in Czechoslovakia are associated in several hundreds of film clubs where important works of world cinema are projected; these works are housed in the vast collection of the Czechoslovak Film Institute.

The short film fulfils important informational, educational and other functions. If we mark the number of short films produced in 1948 with the index 100, in 1960 it is 536.6, and in 1980 it is 1,262.5.

## Television and radio

Both channels of Czechoslovak Television cover the whole country, and a television set is to be found in every household (see Table 30).

On the first channel of Czechoslovak Television, 37 per cent of broadcasting time is devoted to art programmes, i.e. original television drama pro-

TABLE 30.    Development of the number of radio and television licence-holders, 1950–84 (1,000s)

| Year | Radio licence-holders | TV licence-holders | Number of inhabitants per | |
|---|---|---|---|---|
| | | | radio set | TV set |
| 1950 | 2 421 | — | 5.1 | — |
| 1955 | 2 839 | 32 | 4.6 | 409.8 |
| 1960 | 3 104 | 795 | 4.4 | 17.2 |
| 1965 | 3 100 | 2 113 | 4.6 | 6.7 |
| 1970 | 3 174 | 3 091 | 4.5 | 4.6 |
| 1975 | 3 245 | 3 689 | 4.6 | 4.0 |
| 1980 | 4 082 | 4 292 | 3.7 | 3.6 |
| 1981 | 4 099 | 4 296 | 3.7 | 3.6 |
| 1982 | 4 133 | 4 308 | 3.7 | 3.6 |
| 1984 | 4 209 | 4 350 | 3.6 | 3.5 |

TABLE 31.  Development of the structure of telecasting, 1954–83 (in percentages)

| Year | News | Art | Children and youth | Education | Commercials | Other |
|------|------|-----|--------------------|-----------|-------------|-------|
| 1954 | 21.0 | 63.0 | 16.0 | — | — | — |
| 1960 | 49.0 | 32.2 | 14.2 | — | — | — |
| 1965 | 43.1 | 29.2 | 16.1 | — | — | — |
| 1970 | 38.3 | 27.5 | 11.6 | 8.5 | | 14.0 |
| 1975 | 36.6 | 31.4 | 8.9 | 10.3 | 3.8 | 9.0 |
| 1980 | 35.0 | 37.7 | 9.4 | 10.6 | 1.8 | 5.5 |
| 1981 | 31.3 | 42.0 | 9.9 | 10.1 | 1.7 | 5.1 |
| 1982 | 31.3 | 42.1 | 9.6 | 10.2 | 1.7 | 5.1 |
| 1983 | 31.7 | 41.8 | 9.6 | 9.6 | 1.7 | 5.6 |

ductions, television series, adaptations of literary works by Czechoslovak as well as foreign authors, dubbed television plays from foreign networks, films, etc.; 10 per cent to educational programmes; and 9 per cent to programmes for children and youth, most of them also having a cultural character (see Table 31).

Czechoslovak Television presents annually, on average, 170 premières of original television plays, out of which 70 per cent are drama programmes, 16 per cent entertainment programmes, 6 per cent music and drama programmes, and 8 per cent drama programmes for children and youth.

Czechoslovak Television has established an important position in our culture. It does not have a commercial basis (commercials take up only 2 per cent of broadcasting hours) and thus it can concentrate on the dissemination of culture, art and the most recent scientific findings and information.

The attention Czechoslovak Television pays to the quality of its works is also reflected in the number of prizes its programmes are awarded at international competitions and also in the interest from foreign partners in co-operative ventures. From among the prize-winning programmes, mention must be made of the musical film *Romeo and Juliet* and the film *The Golden Eels* which won the Grand Prix at the Prix Italia; the films, *The Witnesses for the Prosecutor*, *Mr Tau*, *Mario and the Magician*, *The Fall of Icarus*, *The Birds of Passage*, *How to Get Dad to the House of Correction* and *A While for the Bugle Song*. They were all awarded prizes at the Golden Nymph International Television Festival in Monte Carlo. *The Dialogue of the Dead* was awarded a prize at the Festival in New York, the musical film *The Pragensia* received the Grand Prix at the same festival, and the programmes *The Lost Revue* and *The Understudies* were awarded prizes in Montreux. Many excellent television films are made for educational or art programmes, for example, *The Growth and Movements of Plants* which received an award at a Festival in Japan, *The Czech Philharmonic Orchestra Plays and Speaks*, and *The Master Works of the National Gallery*, etc.

TABLE 32.　　　　　　　　Development of the structure of radio, 1955–83
(in percentages)

| Year | News | Music programmes | Literary and dramatic programmes | Programmes for children and youth |
|------|------|------------------|----------------------------------|-----------------------------------|
| 1955 | 23.8 | 61.8 | 8.2 | 6.2 |
| 1960 | 25.2 | 60.0 | 8.8 | 6.0 |
| 1965 | 21.4 | 58.0 | 12.8 | 7.8 |
| 1970 | 23.6 | 54.1 | 15.0 | 7.3 |
| 1975 | 24.6 | 56.0 | 10.6 | 7.8 |
| 1980 | 25.0 | 54.7 | 12.3 | 8.0 |
| 1981 | 25.1 | 54.9 | 11.8 | 8.2 |
| 1982 | 24.5 | 54.7 | 12.3 | 8.5 |
| 1983 | 24.7 | 54.5 | 12.4 | 8.4 |

Among world television festivals, the Golden Prague Festival has a prominent place. Television companies from all over the world participate every year, and a similar festival the Prix Danube, is held in Bratislava.

Czechoslovak Radio has a great cultural impact. Radio plays are of a high quality. Music programmes take up 55 per cent of broadcasting time, 12 per cent of broadcasting time is devoted to literary and dramatic programmes, and 8 per cent to programmes for children and youth (see Table 32). In the field of serious music, several programmes were awarded prizes at the International Tribune of Composers (Unesco) and at the Budapest Pro Musica-Olympiada Festival. Recordings and live transmissions from the Prague Spring Festival and the Bratislava Music Festivities, as well as more than 200 other concerts annually, are broadcast by many radio stations abroad. One of the greatest successes for Czechoslovak Radio was the award of the Prix Italia in the 1970s for the musical and dramatic fresco, *Lidice*, by the composer V. Kučera (the RAI State Radio Prize).

## Publishing activity

TABLE 33.　　　　　　　　Non-periodical publishing, 1955–83

| Year | Number of titles | Number of copies (1,000s) |
|------|------------------|---------------------------|
| 1955 | 4 399 | 46 415 |
| 1960 | 6 818 | 48 487 |
| 1965 | 6 503 | 52 822 |
| 1970 | 6 235 | 80 124 |
| 1975 | 6 965 | 79 172 |
| 1980 | 7 324 | 90 412 |
| 1982 | 7 164 | 97 076 |
| 1983 | 7 202 | 98 717 |

TABLE 34. Periodical publishing, 1955–83

| Year | Total periodicals produced | Periodicals produced in the field of culture and art | |
|---|---|---|---|
| | | Titles | Number of copies (1,000s) |
| 1955 | 2 366 | 120 | 80 084 |
| 1960 | 1 222 | 101 | 126 060 |
| 1970 | 1 412 | 237 | 243 257 |
| 1980 | 1 068 | 155 | 274 317 |
| 1982 | 1 070 | 132 | 277 759 |
| 1983 | 1 071 | 132 | 230 216 |

TABLE 35. Music publishing, 1957–82

| Year | Number of titles | Number of copies (1000s) |
|---|---|---|
| 1957 | 395 | 1 141 |
| 1960 | 363 | 1 220 |
| 1965 | 403 | 1 089 |
| 1970 | 397 | 1 128 |
| 1975 | 398 | 1 113 |
| 1980 | 314 | 1 008 |
| 1981 | 334 | 1 034 |
| 1982 | 354 | 1 013 |

## BOOK CLUBS

In 1960, there were in Czechoslovakia five book clubs with 325,000 members who subscribed to 2 million volumes; today Czechoslovakia has fifteen book clubs. The biggest membership is that of the Book Club of the Odeon Publishing House with more than 250,000 members, who since 1953 have subscribed to more than 20 million volumes from among more than 300 titles offered to them. The Club of the Friends of Poetry, with more than 25,000 members, has published over 200 titles over 24 years in 4,300,000 copies.

## CZECHOSLOVAK LITERATURE ABROAD

The authors most translated abroad are: Karel Čapek, Jaroslav Hašek, Julius Fučík, Ivan Olbracht and Božena Němcová. The most frequently translated works by Czech authors are: J. Fučík, *Report from the Gallows* (into 76 languages), and J. Hašek, *The Good Soldier Schweik* (into 31 languages).

## Selling of cultural goods

The Czechoslovak citizen has many opportunities to buy books and works of art in the 971 bookshops, 187 record shops and 30 sales centres of the Czech Fund for Fine Arts, Dílo, the 9 sale-rooms of the Arts and Crafts Centre, and the 15 sale-rooms of the Centre of Folk Art Production.

TABLE 36.      Development of the production of gramophone records (number issued), 1962–80

| 1962 | 1970 | 1975 | 1977 | 1980 |
|---|---|---|---|---|
| 7 375 000 | 9 595 000 | 10 212 000 | 12 458 000 | 14 334 000 |

Out of more than 14 million gramophone records issued every year, almost half are devoted to classical and contemporary serious music.

TABLE 37.      Development of gramophone recordings, 1954–83

| | 1954 | 1960 | 1965 | 1970 | 1975 | 1981 | 1983 |
|---|---|---|---|---|---|---|---|
| Total number of minutes of recording | 5 359 | 5 160 | 7 431 | 10 482 | 10 215 | 10 658 | 16 138 |
| out of which: recordings of | | | | | | | |
| music | 3 950 | 4 751 | 5 349 | 7 453 | 7 659 | 8 472 | 13 427 |
| speech | 768 | 305 | 2 082 | 4 088 | 2 556 | 2 186 | 2 711 |

# International co-operation

There is considerable interest abroad in specific aspects of Czechoslovak cultural policy. For example, the conservation of historic and cultural monuments and the protection of nature are now being extended to the protection of the human environment. There are also the problems of out-of-school education and/or art education, of use of leisure time, of hobbies of many kinds, of editorial policy, etc. A number of foreign experts come every year to Czechoslovakia for study visits and, conversely, Czecho-slovak experts share their experience with many countries of the world. *The preservation of folk culture and folklore* is particularly appreciated. This is not simply a matter of its scientific conservation in museums and specialized institutions, but also of its presentation to a wide public. The folklore dance and song festivals in Strážnice and Východná, in which numerous folklore ensembles from the whole of Europe participate (recently also from Africa and Asia), and which are visited every year by as many as 100,000 spectators, are an opportunity to share these experiences with other countries.

An important place in Czechoslovak foreign relations is held by the Days of Czechoslovak Culture, organized in all socialist countries and also in a number of others (Japan, Portugal, Sweden, Belgium, Finland, etc.). Their objective is to show a cross-section of Czech culture, not just its individual elements.

Czech and Slovak have become subjects of study at a number of universities and colleges throughout the world. Czechoslovakia contributes by sending lecturers in these languages to universities abroad and by organizing Czech-language summer courses at Bratislava University. There is great interest in these courses among students of Slavonic studies abroad. Participants become acquainted in Czechoslovakia, not only with the language, but also with the whole cultural atmosphere. On the lines of these courses, some higher art institutions (particularly those devoted to music) have started to organize *holiday seminars for those interested in the presentation of Czech and Slovak music.* These courses, too, have been well attended for some years now.

The care of important monuments of Czechoslovak history abroad, such as the Hus House in Constance or the Comenius Tomb in Naarden, also come within the province of cultural relations with foreign countries. These places are carefully preserved and the cost is met by the Czechoslovak State.

Cultural relations with foreign countries, the selection of cultural events for Czechoslovakia, as well as their presentation abroad, are carried out according to long-term conceptions, the basis of which are bilateral cultural agreements. Czechoslovakia, as a founder of Unesco, contributes significantly to the work of the Organization and this is demonstrated by the participation of Czechoslovak representatives in different activities and organizations.

Czechoslovakia is a member of the following non-governmental associations and organizations of a cultural character:

European Association of Music Festivals (AEFM)
International Association of Music Libraries (AIBM)
International Amateur Theatre Association (AITA/IATA)
International Association for Children and Youth Theatres (ASSITEJ)
International Bureau of Societies Administering the Rights of Mechanical
    Recording and Reproduction (BIEM)
International Confederation of Societies of Authors and Composers (CISAC)
Confédération Internationale des Sociétés Populaires de Musique (CISPM)
International Federation of Photographic Art
International Board on Books for Young People (IBBY)
International Council of Museums (ICOM)
International Council of Monuments and Sites (ICOMS)
International Federation of Library Associations (IFLA)
International Theatre Institute (ITI)
International Union for Conservation of Nature and Natural Resources (IUCN)
International Organization of Scenographers and Theatre Technicians (OISTT)
International Union of Amateur Cinema (UNICA)
Federation of International Music Competitions (PCIM)
International Federation of Film Archives
International Federation of Film Societies (FICC)
International Federation of Sound Hunters (FICS)
International Federation of the Phonographic Industry
International Federation for Theatre Research
International Society for Violin and Bow-makers
International Music Council (CIM/IMC)
International Music Centre in Vienna
International Confederation of Accordionists (CIA)
International Puppeteers' Union (UNIMA)
Fédération Internationale des Organiseurs des Festivals (FIDOF)
International Association of Transport Museums
International Speleological Union

Internationale Georg F. Händel Gesellschaft (IGFHG)
International Musicological Society (IMS /SIM)
International Society for Music Research
International Copyright Society (INTERGU)
International Union of Technical Cinematographic Associations (UNIATEC)
International Union of Amateur Astronomers (IUAA)
International Union of Directors of Zoological Gardens
International Institute for Conservation of Historic and Artistic Works (ICC)
International Committee of Organizers of Folklore Festivals
National Association for the Protection of Wild Life
Neue Bach-Gesellschaft, Internationale Vereinigung
International Centre for the Study of the Preservation and the Restoration of
    Cultural Property (ICROM)
Association of Special Libraries and Information Bureaux Wild Fowl Trust
    Slimbridge (WFTS)
Verband Deutscher Geigenbauer
World Crafts Council (WCC)
World Accordion Union
Universal Esperanto Asocio
International Jazz Federation (IJF)
International Federation of Photographic Art (FIAP)
International Federation of Medals (FIDEM)
International Academy of Ceramics (AIC)
International Council for Children's Play (ICCP)
International Council of Graphic Design Associations (ICOGRADA)
International Council of Societies of Industrial Design (ICSID)
International Association of Literary Critics (AICL)
International Association of Art Critics (AICA)
International Association of Art, Painting, Sculpture (AIAP)

# Contemporary cultural policy in Czechoslovakia

Programme documents of the Communist Party of Czechoslovakia emphasize the new conception of culture as an essential condition of social progress. The subjective factor (i.e. the individual and his or her abilities, creative activity, morals, education, consciousness, voluntary discipline, and the high level of all activities in the field of work, management, organization, and also the level of social relations) today has a direct influence on socio-economic development. Czechoslovak society has also, in these values, decisive resources for its continued development in the socio-economic field.

In the light of culture's mission and the responsibility stemming from it, devolving primarily on the Department of Culture, the Ministries, as well as other state organs, have paid great attention to the elaboration of conceptual programmes for future cultural development. In these programmes, there was the question of reconciling the need to support basic cultural and political objectives from the point of view of the orientation of the socialist state in internal and foreign policy, with respect for the specificities of the development of individual branches of culture. At the same time, the question of material and technical guarantees of the basic conditions for the fulfilment of these programmes was solved.

In specifying cultural and political objectives, one proceeds from the anticipated movement of society-wide cultural processes. These processes surpass the domain of the Department of Culture and are the concern of society as a whole, requiring co-operation with many other departments, social organizations and the mass media. Without such co-operation, building up the society-wide system of aesthetic education of the population would be unthinkable, as would be the even more important impact on life-style, the development of social planning and the interconnection of the cultural development plan with economic planning.

The basic ideas of this development plan are specified for positive activity in the individual fields of culture.

Art, literature and book culture face a number of tasks, characterized particularly in the field of production by emphazising the qualitative

81

increase in ideological and artistic values. A number of measures are directed towards this goal—for instance, systematic work with young authors, the improvement of the quality of editorial policy with emphasis on publishing original works with contemporary themes, verification of the effectiveness of the existing network of cultural institutions, care for the improvement of the quality of pop music, the solution of problems in co-operation between architects and artists, and the joint enforcement of aesthetic criteria in new housing and urbanization projects. The programme of developments in this sphere includes many tasks with marked priorities.

In the sphere of cultural and educational activity, which includes out-of-school education and hobbies, it is not a matter of single tasks, but of a system with a long-term impact on all groups of society—with special emphasis on the working class and youth—always seeking new differentiated approaches. The programme for the conservation of historic and cultural monuments includes a number of specific tasks through which both the work itself on the preservation of historic buildings, as well as the technical conditions for this activity and the social exploitation of all the preserved values of cultural and educational work, will considerably improve their quality. This is analogically also true for museums and galleries. The protection of nature in the sector falling under the competence of the Ministries of Culture will solve comprehensive problems including legislative, organizational as well as cultural and political questions.

Considerable attention is paid to the economic, organizational, technical, research and staff components of the entire programme. In all cases, the main line of the plan is concretized in specific tasks, proceeding from efforts to achieve the most effective exploitation of available financial means and/or their multiplication in the form of co-operation with extra-departmental institutions. Finally, there are the long-term perspectives such as the character of investment activity, the training of experts, legislative measures and the tasks of technological development.

The programme for the development of the Czech and Slovak cultures requires a transition from departmental approaches to the level of comprehensive planning of society-wide cultural processes. For this, it is necessary to look for possibilities of a greater integration of all cultural institutions, including those outside the framework of the Department of Culture. The fulfilment of this requirement is, of course, no simple matter in the existing conditions and cannot be achieved in a day. Full satisfaction will require a certain time and considerable effort.

The whole programme links the solution of material development with cultural development. It thus contributes to achieving the main objective of the developed socialist society—to bring about the freedom of humanity through many-sided harmonious development. Identification of the objectives of Czechoslovak socialist society in all its aspects enables the cultural policy to focus its attention on synchronizing the social, rational and emotional development of all strata of the population.

# List of institutions

## Czech Socialist Republic

Ministerstvo kultury ČSR (Ministry of Culture of the Czech Socialist Republic), Praha 1, Valdštejnská 10

Ústav pro výzkum kultury (Institute for the Research of Culture), Praha 1, Sněmovní 9

Ústav pro kulturně výchovnou činnost (Institute for the Cultural and Educational Activity), Praha 2, Blanická 4

Výzkumný ústav zvukové, obrazové a reprodukční techniky (Research Institute of Sound, Picture and Reproduction Technology), Praha 5, Plzeňská 66

Institut vzdělávání pracovníků v kultuře a umění (Institute for the Education of Workers in Culture and Art), Praha 3, Škroupovo nám. 9

Ústav pro informace a řízení v kultuře (Institute for Information and Management in Culture), Praha 2, Francouzská 9 Divadelní ústav (Theatre Institute), Praha 1, Celetná 17

Ústředí státní památkové péče a ochrany přírody (Central Office of the State Conservation of Historical and Cultural Monuments and of the Protection of Nature), Praha 1, Valdštejnské nám. 1

Státní ústav památkové péče a ochrany přírody (State Institute of the Conservation of Historical and Cultural Monuments and of the Protection of Nature), Praha 1, Valdštejnské nám. 1

Státní knihovna ČSR (State Library of the Czech Socialist Republic), Praha 1, Klementinum 140

Památník národního písemnictví (National Literature Museum), Praha 1, Strahovské nádvoří 132

Národní galerie (National Gallery), Praha 1, Hradčanské nám. 15 Národní museum (National Museum), Praha 1, Vítězného února 74

Národní technické museum (National Technological Museum), Praha 7, Kostelní 42

Uměleckoprůmyslové museum (Arts and Crafts Museum), Praha 1, 17. listopadu 2

Pragokoncert (Pragokoncert Agency), Praha 1, Maltézské nám. 1

Český fond výtvarných umění (Czech Fund of Fine Arts), Praha 1, Národní 37

Český hudební fond (Czech Music Fund), Praha 1, Besední 3

List of institutions

Český literární fond (Czech Literary Fund) Praha 1, Betlémská 1
Svaz českých dramatických umělců (Union of Czech Dramatic Artists), Praha 1,
Valdštejnské nám. 3
Svaz českých skladatelů a koncertních umělců (Union of Czech Composers
and Concert Artists), Praha 1, Valdštejnské nám. 1
Svaz českých spisovatelů (Union of Czech Writers), Praha 1, Národní 11
Svaz českých výtvarných umělců (Union of Czech Artists), Praha 1, Gottwaldovo
nábř. 250
Dilia—Divadelní a literární agentura (Theatre and Literary Agency), Praha 2,
Vyšehradská 28
OSA—Ochranný svaz autorský pro práva k dílům hudebním (Union for the
Protection of Copyrights for Music Works), Praha 6, Čs. armády 20

## Slovak Socialist Republic

Ministerstvo kultúry SSR (Ministry of Culture of the Slovak Socialist Republic),
Bratislava, Suvorovova 16
Výskumný ústav kultúry (Research Institute of Culture), Bratislava, nám.
Slovenského národného povstania 12
Osvetový ústav (Institute for Adult Education), Bratislava, nám. Slovenského
národného povstania 12
Ústav výchovy a vzdelávania pracovníkov kultúry (Institute for the Education
of Workers in Culture), Bratislava, Lodná 2
Ústav pro informácie a riadenie kultúry (Institute for Information and for
the Management of Culture), Bratislava, Riečna 1
Divadelný ústav (Theatre Institute), Bratislava, Pekárska 7
Ústredie štátnej pamiatkovej starostlivosti (Central Office of the State Conser-
vation of Historical and Cultural Monuments), Bratislava, Hrad
Ústredie štátnej ochrany prírody (Central Office of the State Protection of
Nature), Liptovský Mikuláš, nám. 1. mája 38
Matica slovenská (Slovak Cultural Association—Matica), Martin, Hostihora,
Bratislava, Pugačevova 2
Univerzitna knižnica (University Library), Bratislava, Michalská 1
Ústredná správa muzeí a galérií (Central Administration of Museums and Gal-
leries), Bratislava, Lodná 2
Slovenská národná galéria (Slovak National Gallery), Bratislava, Riečna 1
Slovenské národné múzeum (Slovak National Museum), Bratislava, Vajanského
nábr. 2
Slovkoncert (Slovkoncert Agency), Bratislava, Leningradská 5
Slovenský fond výtvarných umení (Slovak Fund of Fine Arts), Bratislava,
Štúrova 3
Slovenský literárny fond (Slovak Literary Fund), Bratislava, Štúrova 14
Slovenský hudobný fond (Slovak Music Fund), Bratislava, Fučíkova 29
Zväz slovenských spisovateľov (Union of Slovak Writers), Bratislava, Obráncov
mieru 14
Zväz slovenských skladateľov (Union of Slovak Composers), Bratislava, Sládk-
kovičova 11
Zväz slovenských výtvarných umelcov (Union of Slovak Artists), Bratislava,
Obchodné 9/a

Zväz slovenských dramatických umelcov (Union of Slovak Dramatic Artists), Bratislava, Gorkého 4

LITA—Slovenská literárna agentúra (LITA—Slovak Literary Agency), Bratislava, Čs. armády 37/III

Slovenský ochranný zväz autorský pre práva k hudobným dielam (Slovak Union for the Protection of Copyrights for Music Works), Bratislava, Živnostenská 1

Titles in this series: